eat
and two
Veg

Vitality food
with less meat

… for my mother,
who taught me the importance of eating well,
and who knew a thing or two about Yorkshire puddings

eat and two Veg

Vitality food with less meat

Sue Style

Photography by Gus Filgate

David & Charles

Acknowledgements

My thanks go, as ever, to the Badger, tireless supporter and promoter of my puny efforts and seasoned critic of the output, both culinary and literary; to Soph and Oliver, whose love of food (and especially vegetables) has spurred me to ever greater creative efforts; to my cookery students, willing guinea pigs in many an experimental session in my kitchen in Alsace; to Julia Child, Socorro Ramirez, Emile Jung, Michel Husser and Christiane Bisch, each of whom built in their different ways on what my mother started, in teaching me about food.

A DAVID & CHARLES BOOK

First published in the UK in 2001

Copyright text © Sue Style 2001
Copyright photographs © Gus Filgate 2001

Sue Style has asserted her right to be identified
as author of this work in accordance with the Copyright,
Designs and Patents Act, 1988.

A catalogue record for this book is available
from the British Library.

ISBN 0 7153 1010 0

Cookery editor: Anne Sheasby
Photography by Gus Filgate
Food styling by Silvana Franco
Prop styling by Penny Markham
Book design by Judith Robertson

Distributed in the U.S. by
Trafalgar Square, PO Box 257, North Pomfret Vt, 05053
email tsquare@sover.net
www.trafalgarsquarebooks.com

NOTE: Readers in the U.S. should note that additional information about measurement conversions and ingredient equivalents is given on the back flap of the jacket of this book.

Printed in China by Leefung-Asco
for David & Charles
Brunel House   Newton Abbot   Devon

CONTENTS

General Notes

Both metric and imperial measures have been given in all recipes. Use one set of measures only and not a mixture of both.

Standard level spoon measures are used in all recipes.
1 tablespoon = one 15ml spoon
1 teaspoon = one 5ml spoon

Medium eggs should be used except where otherwise specified.

A Note on Fats

Many of the recipes in this book call for olive oil or herb oil (with instructions on making the latter at home). Where cooking methods are concerned, grilling (or barbecuing) is much used, as well as a low-temperature method of roasting/baking meat in the oven (see recipe on page 142), which gives wonderfully succulent results with almost no added fat. Deep-frying is not an option!

As far as dairy fats are concerned, cream and butter are both used, but always judiciously, and whipping cream or crème fraîche is preferred to double cream. Greek yoghurt is also much in evidence (though watch out for the fat content – some are as rich as double cream), as is fromage frais, known in France and Switzerland as fromage blanc. For these there is usually a choice of 40 per cent, 20 per cent or 0 per cent fat: The one with 40 per cent fat is as rich as cream, that with 0 per cent is inedible; my vote goes to the 20 per cent version.

Introduction

One of the most striking trends in today's eating habits is the freedom people feel to compose meals in which meat or fish play only a minor role.

These people are not vegetarians – in fact, they recoil instinctively from the missionary zeal associated with vegetarianism. They are passionately interested in good food based on the best raw materials. They love salads, vegetables, rice, pasta and pulses. Sometimes they enjoy meat, poultry and fish. Desserts for them tend to fall into one of two categories: either simple, fruit-based pleasures, or rather wicked and beautiful indulgences for special occasions.

Such people eat well and simply every day. They entertain in the kitchen, without ceremony, as well as in the dining room. They are young and not so young. They are curious to try new ingredients and are open to influences from foreign cuisines.

This book is for them.

The term 'salad' is used rather loosely in this important first chapter to include a whole range of dishes, some of them exquisitely simple, others beautifully embroidered, all of them way beyond rabbit food. Some of the salads are raw, some cooked and served cold, others are served tiède (lukewarm). There's even a delectable iced soup in there somewhere. Some are first courses, others make light meals or are designed as accompaniments for grilled meats or fish. There are some main-course salads in the poultry and pulses chapters. And in the preserves chapter you'll find ideas on herb oils and vinegars for use in dressings.

Salad has an interesting history. According to Harold McGee (in *On Food and Cooking*), the Greeks were notably fond of lettuce, while the Romans enjoyed a wide range of cold cooked vegetables as hors d'oeuvres. As new foods were discovered and brought to European tables from the New World in the sixteenth century, salad ingredients broadened beyond the rather limited selection of wild and cultivated saladings – herbs, beets, parsnips, cress and the onion family.

John Evelyn, the English gardener-cook, in his book *Acetaria: A Discourse of Sallets* (published in 1699), thrust lettuce into prominence as a salad ingredient, and had plenty of sound advice to give on the correct and most harmonious compositions for salads. During the Age of Enlightenment, the custom in France was to begin a meal with fruit and to end it with salad, the latter being greatly esteemed for its refreshing, digestive, appetite-whetting, anti-aphrodisiac and thirst-quenching qualities. Salad is still generally offered in France after the main course, usually on the same plate to ensure that no good bits of sauce are left lurking. At the beginning of this century, the Swiss learnt to preface almost every meal with salad, thanks to the advice of Dr Bircher-Benner (he of Bircher-Muesli), a practice which persists to this day.

Somewhere along the line, the British lost their taste – and their flair – for the harmoniously balanced salads of Evelyn's day. This is now being remedied both at home and in restaurants, as people's appetite for salads is reawakened, and the average supermarket offers in response a wide range of exciting vegetables and greenery. If you have a garden or allotment, the picture is even better: rocket, oakleaf, lollo, sorrel, lamb's lettuce and many herbs will grow like weeds in the most unpromising plots and save you heaps of money into the bargain.

SALADS
& such

Vinaigrette

Here's a basic vinaigrette that is called for in many recipes. Instructions for making it are printed here to save constant repetition. For oil, use whatever you have to hand according to your preference: a neutral salad oil, olive oil, herb oil or any of the other oils now available.

Vinegars can be anything but malt vinegar – the herb vinegars on page 166 are nice, as are white wine or cider vinegar. A good dose of mustard (not the English, powdered variety) ensures good emulsification; the addition of mayonnaise, yoghurt or hard-boiled egg gives a notably creamy result. A pinch of sugar takes the sharp edge off things – I don't like vinaigrettes that make you choke and your eyes bulge and water.

Make up a batch of vinaigrette and keep it in a jug or screw-top jar in the fridge. Made without mayonnaise, yoghurt or hard-boiled egg, it will keep almost indefinitely; with any of these optional extras, it should be used within 3-4 days. The dressing made with hard-boiled egg will be quite thick, rather like a runny mayonnaise. Thin with a little water, if necessary.

Makes about 500ml (18fl oz) vinaigrette

1 tablespoon French-type **mustard**

1 teaspoon salt

plenty of freshly ground black pepper

300ml (½ pint) **oil**

100ml (3½fl oz) **vinegar**

1 teaspoon **caster sugar**

1 tablespoon **mayonnaise**, or 1 tablespoon natural yoghurt or 1 hard-boiled egg (optional)

Use a liquidizer or hand-held blender to make this dressing. Put all the ingredients in a blender or jug and blend thoroughly until smooth and emulsified. Store in a covered container or sealed jar in the refrigerator.

Aromatic Mushroom Salad with Tomatoes and Ginger

A sort of champignons à la grecque *with oriental overtones, which is lovely for a starter, or as part of a summer buffet. You can substitute other vegetables for mushrooms, sliced in goodish chunks, to great effect – leeks, courgettes, fennel and aubergine all work well.*

Make the herby stock first. Put 300ml (½ pint) water in a wide, heavy-based saucepan with all the ingredients, except the mushrooms and chopped herbs. Bring to the boil, cover and simmer for 10 minutes.

Add the mushrooms, cover again and cook for 10 minutes. Lift out the mushrooms with a slotted spoon and put them in a shallow dish.

Fish out and discard the herbs and chillies, if using. Reduce the juices in the pan by boiling briskly to about half a cupful. Add any juices released by the reclining mushrooms and reduce again. Check and adjust the seasoning, then pour the juices back over the mushrooms. Set aside to cool, then chill them well. Sprinkle with chopped herbs just before serving.

Serves 4

4 tablespoons **olive oil**

juice of 1 **lemon**

salt and freshly ground black pepper

2 **shallots**, finely chopped

1 clove **garlic**, crushed

6-7 fresh **parsley stalks**, a **bay leaf** and a sprig of fresh **thyme**, tied together

1 teaspoon **coriander seeds**, roughly crushed

2 **tomatoes**, skinned and chopped

a walnut-sized piece of **fresh root ginger**, unpeeled and sliced

1-2 fresh red or green **Thai (bird's eye) chillies** (optional)

350g (12oz) **cultivated mushrooms**, whole if small, quartered if not

finely chopped fresh **mixed herbs** such as chervil, chives, parsley and coriander, to garnish

Spicy Iced Pepper Soup with Avocado and Coriander Garnish

This recipe is great for summer – a lovely mixture of Mediterranean and Mexican flavours. The method for skinning peppers (less scary and onerous than you might think) serves as a blueprint for recipes which appear later in the book. Use red or yellow peppers for best results; green are less tasty and give the soup a poor colour.

Heat the oil in a large saucepan and soften the garlic, onion and chilli(es) in the oil without allowing them to brown. Add the stock and simmer for 20 minutes.

Meanwhile, skin the peppers. Put them either in a baking tin in a preheated oven at 240°C/475°F/Gas Mark 9, or under a hot grill, or directly over a gas flame. Roast or grill them until thoroughly blistered and quite black, stopping short of complete incineration. Turn them regularly to ensure even searing.

Remove from the heat, put the peppers in a plastic bag and leave to sweat for 10 minutes (this continues the cooking so that they soften nicely – important for this recipe in which the peppers get little further cooking). Rub off the skins and rinse the peppers under running water. Remove and discard the stalks and seeds and cut the flesh into pieces. Add the pepper flesh to the stock and simmer for 5 minutes.

Remove the pan from the heat, cool the soup a little, then add the crème fraîche and purée the mixture in a blender or food processor until perfectly smooth. Check and adjust the seasoning if necessary – the soup can afford to be quite highly seasoned as it will be served cold. Set aside to cool, then chill the soup before serving. To serve, divide among 6 bowls and garnish with avocado and fresh coriander leaves.

Serves 6

2 tablespoons **olive oil**

2 cloves **garlic**, crushed

1 **onion**, finely chopped

1-2 fresh **green chillies** such as serrano, jalapeño or peperoncini, deseeded and finely chopped

1.5 litres (2¾ pints) **chicken stock**

2 **red** or **yellow peppers**

250ml (9fl oz) **crème fraîche**

salt and freshly ground black pepper

1 **avocado**, peeled, stoned and cut into slices or cubes and fresh **coriander** leaves, to garnish

Aubergine, Tomato and Goat's Cheese 'Stacks' with Pesto

An excellent, speedy starter consisting of grilled aubergines, tomatoes and sliced goat's cheese spread with pesto, piled up in a stack and set over a bed of salad leaves. Ideally, the aubergines, tomatoes and goat's cheese should be about the same diameter, otherwise your 'stacks' will be a little lopsided. Use courgettes instead of aubergines if you prefer.

Serves 8

2 medium-sized **aubergines**, about 350g (12oz) each

salt

herb oil (see recipes on page 168) or other oil, for brushing

8 small fresh **goat's cheeses**, such as Chèvretines, about 20g (¾oz) each or 200g (7oz) goat's cheese

4 teaspoons **pesto**

4 small **tomatoes**, sliced

a little **vinaigrette** (see recipe on page 10) or basil and garlic oil (see recipe on page 168)

mixed **salad leaves** such as oakleaf, rocket and radicchio, to serve

---

Preheat the grill to high. Slice the aubergines into 1cm (½in) slices and put them on a lightly oiled, heavy baking sheet (or put them on the rack of a grill pan). Sprinkle the slices with a little salt, brush with oil and grill on one side until lightly golden – about 2-3 minutes, depending on your heat source. Watch them carefully and do not allow them to burn. Turn them over, brush with oil again and grill the second side until lightly golden. Remove from the heat.

Cut the small goat's cheeses in half horizontally (or slice the goat's cheese into 1cm/½in slices). Assemble the 'stacks' using in each case a slice of aubergine, a slice of goat's cheese, a little pesto and a slice of tomato; repeat these layers and finish with an aubergine slice.

Put the 'stacks' on serving plates and drizzle a little vinaigrette or basil and garlic oil on top. Surround them with mixed salad leaves tossed in vinaigrette and serve with Herby Flat Bread (see recipe on page 155) or the Courgette and Basil Bread (see page 158).

Upside-Down Avocados with Cream Cheese and Walnuts on Rocket Salad

Avocados are definitely not a low-fat food (they contain around 25 per cent fat) but they are extremely nutritious. They contain the highest protein content of any fruit, as well as being rich in vitamins A and B. So, while keeping in mind that they are extremely calorific, we can comfort ourselves that they are Very Good for Us. In this super-simple starter, the avocados are halved and stoned, and the skin peeled away. The cavity is filled with low-fat cream cheese and chopped walnuts, drizzled with a walnut oil dressing and served over a rocket salad.

Serves 6

FOR THE SALAD

3 avocados

18 walnut halves

150g (5½oz) low-fat cream cheese

rocket leaves, to serve

FOR THE DRESSING

6 tablespoons walnut oil

2 tablespoons white wine vinegar

salt and freshly ground black pepper

1 teaspoon French-type mustard

a pinch of caster sugar

For the salad, halve the avocados, remove the stones and peel away the skin carefully. Roughly chop 12 walnut halves and mix them with the cream cheese. Fill the avocado cavities with the mixture and invert them onto rocket leaves laid on serving plates.

Put all the dressing ingredients in a small bowl or screw-top jar and whisk or shake the them together until thoroughly mixed. Spoon the dressing over the avocados, garnish with the remaining walnut halves and serve immediately.

Avocado and Bacon Ciabatta Sandwiches

Wonderful for lunch with (or after) a bowl of soup. The ciabatta bread is split and filled with an irresistible mixture of smooth avocado slices, crispy bacon, a little lettuce and a delicious mustardy mayonnaise.

Fry the bacon rashers in a frying pan, without extra fat, until golden brown and crispy. Drain on absorbent kitchen paper.

Split the ciabatta loaves in half lengthways. Mix the mayonnaise with the mustard and spread it on the ciabatta halves, top and bottom.

Cut the lettuce leaves to fit and lay some on the ciabatta 'bottoms'. Top with the bacon rashers and avocado slices. Finish with more lettuce and top with the other ciabatta halves. Cut each 'sandwich' into manageable portions and serve.

Makes 6 sandwiches

12 rashers **streaky bacon**, preferably dry-cured

2 loaves of **ciabatta bread**, each weighing about 275g (9¾oz)

6 tablespoons **mayonnaise**

1 tablespoon **green mustard with herbs** (or add 2 tablespoons finely chopped fresh herbs such as chives, parsley and chervil to 1 tablespoon French mustard)

6 large crispy **lettuce leaves**

1 **avocado**, peeled, stoned and sliced

Salade Tiède of Asparagus, Mushrooms, Peppers and Tomatoes

A recipe created by my son at the height of the asparagus season, which coincided with an intensive recipe-testing phase. It's as delicious as it is beautiful. Serve as a starter, or with grilled fish, poultry or meat; or as a light main course.

Cook the asparagus in a pan of boiling, salted water until barely tender – about 8-12 minutes, depending on thickness. Drain, reserving the water. Cut the spears in half crossways and reserve the tips. Put the bottom asparagus halves in a blender or food processor with the vinaigrette. Blend until smooth, using a little of the reserved cooking water to thin the dressing to a pouring consistency. Set aside.

Heat the oil in a heavy-based frying pan and soften the onion and garlic gently in the oil without allowing them to brown. Add the mushrooms and lemon juice, season to taste with salt and pepper, then cover and cook gently until the mushrooms exude plenty of juice.

Uncover, increase the heat and cook briskly to drive off excess moisture, stirring occasionally. Toss in the pepper chunks, tomato quarters and lemon grass, if using. Continue to cook, stirring, for a further 2-3 minutes. Finally, stir in the asparagus tips and heat through briefly. Stir in the chopped parsley.

Arrange the hot salad decoratively on 4 plates and spoon the dressing over the salad.

Serves 4 as a starter or **Serves 2-3** as a light main dish

500g (1lb 2oz) fresh **green asparagus**, trimmed

salt and freshly ground black pepper

4 tablespoons **vinaigrette** (see recipe on page 10)

1 tablespoon **olive oil**

1 small **onion**, chopped

3 cloves **garlic**, crushed

300g (10½oz) **mushrooms**, sliced, or quartered if large

juice of ½ **lemon**

½ large **green pepper**, grilled, skinned, deseeded and cut into chunks (see page 13)

200g (7oz) **tomatoes**, skinned, deseeded and quartered

a pinch of powdered **lemon grass** (optional)

plenty of roughly chopped fresh flat-leaf **parsley**

Ceviches of Marinated Salmon with Courgettes and Avocado Dressing

Ceviche is a Mexican dish of marinated mackerel and avocado seasoned with coriander and chilli. Here's a fresh interpretation made with salmon, packed into courgette-lined ramekins and served with an avocado dressing. Serve with warm brown bread rolls or tortilla chips.

Serves 8

800g (1¾lb) skinless, boneless **salmon fillet**

salt and freshly ground black pepper

juice of 2 **lemons** or 3 limes (about 100ml/3½fl oz)

2 tablespoons **olive oil** or chilli oil

(see recipe on page 168)

4 tablespoons **salad oil**

1-2 fresh **green chillies** such as serrano, jalapeño or peperoncini, deseeded and finely chopped

1 **shallot**, finely chopped

plenty of chopped fresh **coriander**

1 **courgette**

1 **avocado**, peeled, stoned and cut into small cubes

fresh **coriander** sprigs, to garnish

Trim the salmon of any greyish, fatty parts near the backbone, and any remaining skin; run your finger down the fish to make sure there are no bones lurking, extracting them with tweezers. Cut the fish into small dice and put it in a shallow, non-metallic dish with the salt and pepper, lemon or lime juice, olive or chilli oil, salad oil, chillies, shallot and chopped coriander and stir to mix. Cover and refrigerate for several hours or overnight – the fish will become opaque as it marinates.

Cut the courgette into wafer-thin slices, lay the slices on absorbent kitchen paper, salt lightly and cover with more absorbent kitchen paper. Leave for a while for the salt to draw out the juices, then pat dry.

Tip the marinated fish into a colander over a bowl and reserve and refrigerate the strained juices. Brush eight 7-8cm (2¾-3¼in) ramekin dishes with a little olive oil. Line the bottom and sides of each ramekin with courgette slices. Pack the strained ceviche into each ramekin, pressing down well with the back of a spoon. Cover and refrigerate for at least 4 hours and up to 24 hours.

Shortly before serving, put the reserved juices in a food processor with the avocado flesh and blend to make a smooth dressing. Thin the dressing to a pouring consistency, if necessary, by blending in a little water. Run a knife round the ramekins and turn out the ceviches onto serving plates. Garnish with coriander sprigs and serve with the avocado dressing drizzled over.

Courgette Carpaccio

A beautiful summer starter consisting of concentric circles of wafer-thin slices of green and yellow courgettes sprinkled with salt, oil and shaved parmesan. If you can't find or haven't grown yellow courgettes, use all green ones.

To slice the courgettes very thinly, use a food processor with slicing disc fitted, or a mandoline slicer. Otherwise, cut the courgettes into wafer-thin slices with a sharp knife and arrange them in concentric circles and alternating colours on 4 plates.

Sprinkle with salt and pepper and drizzle with oil. Add shavings of parmesan cheese and garnish with nasturtium flowers, if liked.

Chill until required, but serve promptly after preparation, otherwise the courgettes will become limp and tired.

Serves 4

1 medium **yellow courgette**, about 125g (4½oz) in weight

1 medium **green courgette**, about 125g (4½oz) in weight

coarse salt and freshly ground black pepper

4 tablespoons **olive oil** or herb oil (see recipes on page 168)

parmesan cheese shavings, to serve

nasturtium flowers, to garnish (optional)

Salad of Red Onions, White Cheese and Green Peppers

Normally I'm not very keen on both raw onions and peppers in a salad – they tend to come back at you for hours afterwards. In this case, both are lightly grilled, and the peppers are skinned which makes them more digestible and adds to their flavour. The sweetness of the balsamic vinegar gives a nice counterpoint to the other ingredients. A salad of good colour and texture contrasts.

Serves 4

3 tablespoons **olive oil**, plus extra for brushing

1 tablespoon **balsamic vinegar**

salt and freshly ground black pepper

4 **red onions**, thickly sliced

1 **green pepper**, grilled, skinned, deseeded and cut into strips
(see page 13)

100g (3½oz) **feta cheese**, crumbled or diced

fresh flat-leaf **parsley** leaves, to garnish

In a mixing bowl, whisk together the oil, vinegar and salt and pepper for the dressing. Set aside.

Preheat the grill to high. Put the onion slices on a lightly oiled piece of foil and brush them with a little more oil. Grill the onion slices until lightly charred, turning over once.

Separate the slices into rings and put them into the mixing bowl, turning to coat with the dressing. Lift out with a slotted spoon and arrange them on a large serving plate.

Toss the pepper strips in the dressing, lift out with a slotted spoon and drape them over the onion rings. Top with the feta cheese, drizzle any remaining dressing over the top and garnish with parsley leaves.

Bündnerfleisch 'Millefeuilles' with Cream Cheese and Walnuts

I came up with this rather wicked starter in response to a group of cookery students who wanted a menu combining raw materials from both Switzerland and Alsace (the two areas on our doorstep). It consists of air-dried beef (Bündnerfleisch) layered with cream cheese and chopped walnuts, briefly frozen until firm enough to cut, and served over a seasonal salad.

Put 12 walnut halves in a food processor and chop finely. Add the cream cheese and cottage cheese and process until smooth.

Lay a slice of Bündnerfleisch or air-dried beef on a sheet of foil, spread some of the cheese mixture over the beef and top this with another slice of beef. Continue in this way until half of the cheese mixture and half of the beef slices are used up. Wrap the stack in the foil to make a neat rectangular parcel.

Repeat with the remaining beef slices and cheese filling to make a second stack. Put the stacks in the freezer for 1-2 hours to firm up and to facilitate slicing.

Remove the stacks from the freezer, unwrap and discard the foil, then, using a very sharp knife, cut each stack into 8 slices. Arrange a rosette of lamb's lettuce or other salad leaves on serving plates, lay 2 slices of 'millefeuilles' on top and garnish each slice with a walnut half. Garnish with an avocado segment and drizzle with a little walnut oil.

Serves 8

28 **walnut halves**, preferably freshly shelled

150g (5½oz) **low-fat cream cheese**

150g (5½oz) **cottage cheese**

100g (3½oz) **Bündnerfleisch** or **air-dried beef** (about 20 slices)

a handful of **lamb's lettuce** or other salad leaves

1 **avocado**, peeled, stoned and cut into 8 segments

walnut oil, for drizzling

Feta Mousses with Black Olives and Tomatoes

This quick and easy starter full of Mediterranean flavours – an appealing variation on the Greek Salad theme – consists of small white castles of lightly set feta garnished with black olives and tomato strips. As the feta itself is very salty, it is important to use unsalted stock – this rules out stock cubes in which salt is the chief component.

Serves 6

4 sheets **gelatine** or
2 teaspoons powdered gelatine

250ml (9fl oz) unsalted **chicken** or **vegetable stock** (see note above)

200g (7oz) **feta cheese**

250ml (9fl oz) **whipping cream**

freshly ground black pepper (and salt if needed)

2 **tomatoes**, halved, deseeded and cut into strips

black olives, to serve

3-4 tablespoons **vinaigrette** (see recipe on page 10)

fresh flat-leaf **parsley** sprigs, to garnish

Soften the gelatine sheets in a bowl of cold water until floppy. Heat the stock in a pan to just below boiling point and drop in the squeezed-out gelatine. Remove the pan from the heat and stir well until the gelatine has dissolved. Alternatively, sprinkle the powdered gelatine onto the stock in a small pan, leave until spongy, then heat gently, stirring until dissolved.

Put the feta cheese and cream into a blender or food processor, add the hot gelatine and blend until smooth. Season with black pepper – you probably won't need salt but taste to see.

Lightly oil six 7-8cm (2¾-3¼in) ramekin dishes, divide the feta mixture evenly among them and level the surfaces. Chill for several hours until set.

Turn out the mousses onto serving plates. Surround each mousse with tomato strips and black olives, drizzle some vinaigrette over and garnish with parsley sprigs.

'Guacamole' and Smoked Salmon Mousses on a Bed of Salad Leaves

For this lovely 'new-Mexican' starter, think guacamole for the flavourings; skip the mayonnaise and double cream of the old-wave avocado mousses in favour of Greek yoghurt and crème fraîche and pour it into smoked salmon-lined ramekins.

Makes 6 mousses

4 sheets **gelatine** or
2 teaspoons powdered
gelatine

150ml (¼ pint) **chicken**
or **vegetable stock**

1 **avocado**, peeled,
stoned and diced

1-2 fresh **green chilli(es)**,
deseeded and chopped

1-2 tablespoons chopped
fresh **coriander**

juice of 1 **lime** or lemon

salt and freshly ground
black pepper

a splash of **Tabasco sauce**
(optional)

4 tablespoons
crème fraîche

150ml (¼ pint)
Greek yoghurt

6 small slices **smoked
salmon**, about 200g
(7oz) in total weight

dressed **salad leaves** and
a little finely chopped
onion, to garnish

Soak the gelatine sheets in a bowl of cold water until floppy. Squeeze them out and dissolve them gently in a small pan with the stock. Alternatively, sprinkle the powdered gelatine onto the stock in a small pan, leave until spongy, then heat gently, stirring until dissolved.

Put the avocado flesh in a blender or food processor with the finely chopped chilli(es), coriander, lime or lemon juice, salt and pepper, Tabasco, if using, crème fraîche, Greek yoghurt and the hot gelatine and stock mixture. Blend until smooth and well mixed. Check and adjust the seasoning.

Line six 7-8 cm (2¾-3¼in) ramekin dishes with the smoked salmon slices. Pour in the avocado mixture, then chill for several hours or overnight until set.

Run a knife round the ramekins and turn them out onto serving plates. Garnish with some dressed salad leaves and chopped onion.

Pancetta and Cream Cheese 'Snails' on a Bed of Salad Leaves

Herby crêpes are spread with low-fat cream cheese, overlaid with pancetta (or prosciutto or smoked salmon, if you prefer), rolled up and served sliced over a salad.

Spread the cold crêpes thinly with the cream cheese and lay the pancetta slices on top. Roll up the crêpes tightly, place them on a plate and chill them in the freezer for about 30 minutes, or until 'rigor mortis' is just setting in.

Remove from the freezer and slice them into 2cm (¾in) slices on a slant. Divide the dressed salad leaves among 6 plates and arrange the crêpe spirals on top.

Serves 6

3 cooked cold **herby crêpes**
(see recipe on page 34)

125g (4½oz) **low-fat cream cheese**

100g (3½oz) **pancetta,** thinly sliced

assorted dressed **salad leaves** such as oakleaf, lollo rosso and rocket

Lamb's Lettuce, Chicory, Camembert and Walnut Salad

A good salad for winter, and one with excellent colour and texture contrasts.

Divide the chicory into leaves and arrange them on 2 plates or in 2 soup bowls. Put a 'nest' of lamb's lettuce in the middle, arrange the camembert wedges over the lettuce and garnish with walnut halves. Spoon the vinaigrette over the salad and serve.

Serves 2

1 head **chicory**

two good handfuls of **lamb's lettuce** (about 50g/1¾oz)

about 100g (3½oz) **camembert,** cut into wedges

10 **walnut halves**

4-5 tablespoons **vinaigrette**
(see recipe on page 10)

Smoked Duck Breast and Avocado Salad with Toasted Pumpkin Seeds

Smoked duck breast, vacuum-packed, is getting easier to find. Remove and discard the fat, splay the slivers of meat out over a mixture of leaves and garnish with avocado. The fat may be diced small, dry-fried until golden and crusty and scattered over to give the salad a delicious and crunchy garnish.

Serves 4

2 tablespoons hulled (green) **pumpkin seeds**

4 good handfuls of mixed **salad leaves**

2 **avocados**

100g (3½oz) **smoked duck breast**, sliced

150ml (¼ pint) **vinaigrette**
(see recipe on page 10)

fresh **chervil** sprigs and **edible flowers**, to garnish (optional)

Preheat the oven to 200°C/400°F/Gas Mark 6. Spread the pumpkin seeds out on a baking sheet and cook in the oven for about 10 minutes or until lightly coloured and fragrant – do not allow them to burn. Remove from the oven and set aside.

Divide the salad leaves among 4 plates. Peel and halve the avocados and remove and discard the stones. Cut each avocado half into 4 wedges and arrange these decoratively with the duck breast slices over the salad leaves.

Drizzle the vinaigrette over the avocado and duck and scatter the pumpkin seeds on top. Garnish with chervil sprigs and edible flowers, if liked.

Beetroot and Fresh Goat's Cheese Terrine

Even if you think you don't like beetroot – or, for that matter, goat's cheese – you should try this beautiful 'terrine'. The sweetness of the beets is offset by the sharp freshness of the goat's cheese, and the colour contrast is very appealing. It is extremely quick to assemble and for some miraculous reason it even holds together when sliced. If you'd rather not make a terrine, simply place 'stacks' of alternating beetroot and creamy, soft goat's cheese slices on serving plates on a pool of green dressing, and garnish with salad leaves.

Makes 14–16 slices (Serves 8–10)

olive oil, for brushing

500g (1lb 2oz) cooked, peeled **beetroots**, cut into ½cm (¼in) slices

500g (1lb 2oz) fresh, soft **goat's cheese**, cut into ½cm (¼in) slices

coarse salt and freshly ground black pepper

FOR THE GREEN HERBY DRESSING

150ml (¼ pint) **olive oil**

3 tablespoons **white wine vinegar**

1 tablespoon **green herby mustard** (or add 2 tablespoons finely chopped fresh herbs such as chives, parsley and chervil to 1 tablespoon French mustard)

1 tablespoon **mayonnaise**

a pinch of **caster sugar**

Brush a 28x10x8cm (11x4x3¼in) terrine or loaf tin with oil and line with cling wrap (the oil helps the cling wrap to hold to the sides). Arrange slices of beetroot and goat's cheese in alternate layers in the prepared tin, seasoning with a little salt and pepper as you go. Press down quite firmly and close the cling wrap over the top. Place a weight on top, such as a can of soup or beans. Refrigerate for at least 12 hours.

For the dressing, put the oil, vinegar, mustard (and herbs if used), mayonnaise, sugar into a blender or food processor, season with salt and pepper, and purée together to make a smooth green emulsion.

Turn the terrine out onto a board, remove and discard the cling wrap and slice the terrine carefully. Pour a little dressing onto each serving plate and lay 2 slices of terrine over the dressing.

Boulgour Salad with Avocado, Tomatoes and Herbs

This nutty salad of boulgour (also known as bulgur or burghul) with tomatoes, avocado and lemon juice has an earthy, peasant flavour and great texture. It is extraordinarily good with cold meats, especially lamb.

Heat 2 tablespoons oil in a saucepan and soften the onion in the oil without allowing it to brown. Add the boulgour and cook for 10 minutes, stirring.

Dissolve the stock cube in 500ml (18fl oz) boiling water. Add this to the boulgour, stir to mix, then cover the pan and remove it from the heat. Leave for 10 minutes, by which time all the liquid should be absorbed. Fork up the boulgour and season to taste with salt and pepper.

Turn the boulgour into a bowl. Stir in the remaining oil, the tomatoes, avocado, lemon juice and chopped herbs, mixing well. Set aside to cool, then chill the salad before serving.

Serves 6-8

5 tablespoons **olive oil**

1 **onion**, finely chopped

250g (9oz) quick-cook **boulgour**

1 **vegetable stock cube**

salt and freshly ground black pepper

2 **tomatoes**, finely chopped

1 **avocado**, peeled, stoned and diced

juice of 1 **lemon**

plenty of chopped fresh **mixed herbs** such as lovage, chives and wild garlic leaves

Tomato Mousses with Quail's Eggs

The base of this Mediterranean-Mexican starter is a well-flavoured, mildly creamy tomato sauce, lightly set with gelatine. A quail's egg is buried inside each mousse. Turn the mousses out and garnish with halved quail's eggs and some salad leaves.

Boil the quail's eggs – put them in a pan of cold water and bring to the boil for 3 minutes, then drain and put them in cold water to stop the cooking. Peel them and set aside.

For the tomato sauce, skin the tomatoes and chop them roughly. Heat the oil in a pan and soften the onion, garlic and chilli in the oil without allowing them to brown.

Add the tomato flesh and salt and pepper and add a little sugar to taste (depending on the acidity of the tomatoes). Add the thyme, cover the pan and cook over a moderate heat until the sauce base is well-flavoured and somewhat reduced, stirring occasionally.

Remove the pan from the heat and press the sauce through a sieve into a bowl, to remove the seeds, thyme and so on. Whisk the crème fraîche into the tomato sauce and set aside.

Heat the stock in a pan to just below boiling point. Squeeze out the gelatine sheets, drop them into the hot stock and stir until dissolved. Alternatively, add the soaked, powdered gelatine to the hot stock and stir until dissolved. Mix this into the tomato sauce and set aside.

Lightly brush ten 7-8cm (2¾-3¼in) ramekin dishes with oil. Put a quail's egg in each one and fill with the tomato mixture. Cool, then chill for several hours until set.

To serve, run a knife round the mousses and turn them out onto serving plates. Garnish with dressed salad leaves and the remaining quail's eggs, halved.

Serves 10

20 **quail's eggs**

200ml (7fl oz) **chicken stock**

6 sheets **gelatine**, soaked in cold water or 1 tablespoon powdered gelatine, sprinkled over 3 tablespoons cold water

FOR THE TOMATO SAUCE

1kg (2¼lb) **tomatoes**

1 tablespoon **olive oil**

1 **onion**, finely chopped

1 clove **garlic**, crushed

1 fresh **green chilli** such as serrano, jalapeño or peperoncini, deseeded and finely chopped

salt and freshly ground black pepper

1-2 teaspoons **caster sugar**, or to taste

a sprig of fresh **thyme**

3 tablespoons **crème fraîche**

dressed **salad leaves**, to garnish

Warm Salad of Fleischschnacka and Wild Mushrooms

Fleischschnacka (literally 'meat snails') are a traditional Alsace dish, consisting of minced meat rolled up strudel-wise in pasta dough or pastry and sliced into spirals – hence the snail allusion. In this reinterpretation, a chicken liver and bacon filling is rolled up in herby crêpes, which are sliced, fried and served with wild mushrooms. It makes a wonderful autumnal starter or supper dish. For spring or summer, serve the fleischschnacka on a bed of dressed salad leaves.

Serves 6-8

FOR THE HERBY CRÊPES
125ml (4fl oz) **milk**
125g (4½oz) **plain flour**
pinch of salt
2 tablespoons **olive oil**
2 **eggs**
a handful of fresh **herbs**
in season, chopped

FOR THE FLEISCHSCHNACKA
200g (7oz) **lardons** or
streaky bacon, chopped
400g (14oz) **chicken
livers**, trimmed and
chopped
salt and freshly ground
black pepper
2 **eggs**
2-3 tablespoons
whipping cream
olive oil, for frying

(continued on opposite page)

Make the herby crêpes. Put all the ingredients for the crêpes in a blender or food processor. Add 125ml (4fl oz) water and blend until smooth and well mixed.

Brush an 18cm (7in) crêpe pan with a little oil and heat it steadily. Pour about a tablespoonful of the crêpe mixture into the pan, tilting the pan so that the bottom is just coated. Cook until the underside is golden, then turn or toss the crêpe and cook the second side.

Put the cooked crêpe on a plate. Repeat with the remaining batter (there should be just enough mixture to make 10 thin crêpes), stacking the cooked crêpes up on the plate as they are ready. Set aside.

For the fleischschnacka, fry the lardons or bacon in a frying pan until lightly golden, stirring occasionally. Increase the heat, add the chicken livers, season to taste with salt and pepper and fry briskly, tossing and turning them, until the livers are just stiffened.

Scrape the contents of the pan into a blender or food processor, add the eggs and cream and blend roughly to mix. Divide the mixture even between the crêpes, spreading it thinly almost to the edges. Roll the crêpes up tightly, set aside to cool, then chill until firm.

Slice them on a slant, discarding the end pieces. Heat a little oil in a frying pan and fry the crêpe slices cut sides downwards until lightly golden, turning them once. Remove from the pan, place on a plate and keep warm.

In the same pan, heat a little oil and fry the mushrooms for 4-5 minutes or until just cooked. Add 2-3 tablespoons of vinegar and cook briskly until almost reduced, stirring frequently.

To serve, put a little heap of mushrooms in the middle of each plate and arrange the fleischschnacka (fried crêpe slices) around them. Garnish with herb sprigs and sprinkle with a few more drops of vinegar.

300g (10½oz) assorted **wild mushrooms**

2-3 tablespoons Melfor or **balsamic vinegar**, plus a little extra for sprinkling

fresh **herb** sprigs, to garnish

Vegetables are wonderful food, and are all too often sorely mistreated. Their textures are endlessly varied, their flavours complex. Cooks can be ceaselessly creative with them. (The fact that they are good for us should, I think, be soft-pedalled; such labelling is the kiss of death for any food.)

The following is an eclectic collection of lively dishes – the choice of raw ingredients has been an entirely arbitrary process, dictated by personal likes and dislikes, and by what I can grow in my own garden or buy locally. Your selection and tastes may be different, so where possible or appropriate I have simply specified a given amount of any mixed vegetables.

Many of the resulting dishes can stand proudly alone, while others can play a starring role alongside grilled meat or fish. Some, like the vegetable strudel or polenta layered with blue cheese and walnuts, are real party pieces, while others make excellent light supper or lunch dishes.

VEGETABLES & things

Herby Roast Vegetables

*I*n this simple but delicious recipe, assorted vegetables are cut into batons, arranged in a large roasting tin, anointed with oil and roasted for 25-30 minutes. It's good if you have plenty of different colours, and also if you use a herb-infused oil. The vegetables, lightly golden but still crunchy-tender, retain all their goodness and flavour cooked in this way. I find roast vegetables more reliable than grilled, which are apt to burn the minute you turn your back. They also cook more evenly. Serve them without ceremony, straight from the roasting tin, or toss them with dressing in a large bowl and serve at room temperature.

Serves 8-10

about 2kg (4½lb)
assorted vegetables
such as fennel, carrots, courgettes, leeks (with some green left on), celeriac and potatoes

salt and freshly ground black pepper

olive oil or herb oil
(see recipes on page 168), for drizzling

finely chopped fresh **mixed herbs** such as lovage, parsley and tarragon

vinaigrette
(see recipe on page 10), if serving the vegetables as a salad (optional)

Line a large 40x30cm (16x12in) or similar size roasting tin with foil. Trim and/or peel the vegetables and cut into strips about the size of your little finger, then arrange the vegetables in the prepared tin, alternating the colours and seasoning lightly with salt and pepper as you go. The vegetables can be prepared ahead and refrigerated for several hours, or overnight, covered with a damp teatowel.

Preheat the oven to 220°C/425°F/Gas Mark 7. Drizzle the vegetables with oil, then roast them in the oven for 25-35 minutes, until the top ones are lightly browned and the bulk are just cooked, but still a little crunchy.

Fish some out to taste and continue to cook a little longer, if necessary.

Sprinkle with chopped herbs and serve straight from the tin. Alternatively, tip them into a large bowl, sprinkle with herbs and toss them with some vinaigrette before serving.

Veggie Toad (in the Hole)

A sort of clafoutis of seasonal vegetables baked in a Yorkshire pudding batter. The vegetables will vary according to what is available, and they can be grilled, roasted or barbecued rather than pan-fried, if this suits you better.

Serves 6

125ml (4fl oz) **milk**

salt and freshly ground black pepper

100g (3½oz) **plain flour**

4 **eggs**

1 tablespoon **olive oil**, plus extra for cooking

300g (10½oz) **mushrooms**

300g (10½oz) **aubergines**

2 **leeks**, about 200g (7oz) in weight, washed

1 teaspoon **garam masala** or other mixture of ground spices

Put the milk in a bowl with 125ml (4fl oz) water, a pinch of salt, the flour, eggs and 1 tablespoon oil and whisk together to make a smooth batter. Set aside.

If the mushrooms are small, leave them whole, otherwise cut them into quarters. Cut the aubergines and leeks into similar-sized chunks.

Heat a little oil in a frying pan and fry the mushrooms with salt and pepper to taste, until lightly browned. Remove the pan from the heat, tip the mushrooms into a bowl and set aside. Preheat the oven to 220°C/425°F/Gas Mark 7.

Fry the aubergines in the same pan, adding a little more oil if necessary, until lightly golden, turning occasionally. Season to taste with salt and pepper and add them to the mushrooms.

Finally, cook the leeks briskly in the frying pan for 4-5 minutes, adding 2-3 tablespoons of water to the pan and stirring occasionally – they should remain crunchy. Mix the vegetables together in the bowl with the garam masala or spices.

Lightly oil a 30x25cm (12x10in) or similar size roasting tin and put it in the oven to get thoroughly hot. Pour in the batter, then add the prepared vegetables, pushing them down into the batter. Bake in the oven for about 25 minutes or until golden and billowy, and the vegetables are just cooked.

Mixed Vegetable Couscous with Garam Masala

This colourful and delicious dish can be prepared entirely in advance and can be served on its own or as an accompaniment to a meat or fish dish. Buy garam masala ready-made, or make your own: using a pestle and mortar, grind together 2 teaspoons black peppercorns, 4 teaspoons coriander seeds, 4 teaspoons cumin seeds, 1 clove and a 1cm (½in) piece of cinnamon stick.

Preheat the oven to 150°C/300°F/Gas Mark 2. Trim and/or peel the vegetables and cut them into small pieces, or 'turn' them into neat ovals if you have the patience and the inclination. Put them in a saucepan with water barely to cover, 1 tablespoon oil and salt and pepper to taste. Cook until just tender, about 5-6 minutes, depending on size and maturity.

Tip the vegetables into a colander or strainer held over a measuring jug. Make up the cooking water to 500ml (18fl oz), return it to the pan with salt and pepper and the remaining oil. Bring back to the boil, then pour in the couscous in a steady stream, stirring.

Remove the pan from the heat and fork the couscous up to mix well. Stir in the vegetables, mixing well, then turn the mixture into a lightly oiled ovenproof dish. Cover with foil and bake in the oven for 15-20 minutes. Just before serving, stir in the garam masala.

Serves 8

500g (1lb 2oz) **mixed vegetables** in season such as baby carrots, baby turnips and courgettes

2 tablespoons **olive oil**

salt and freshly ground black pepper

500g (1lb 2oz) medium-fine pre-cooked **couscous**

2 teaspoons **garam masala**, or to taste

Courgette 'Rösti' with Fresh Goat's Cheese, Cherry Tomatoes and Herbs

If your courgettes get a bit above themselves and turn into marrows, use them in this delicious dish. The flesh is grated, salted and squeezed dry, mixed with shallot and herbs and fried like a Rösti. The topping is of soft goat's cheese and cherry tomatoes.

Serves 4-6

500g (1lb 2oz) **courgettes**

about 2 teaspoons salt

3 **eggs**

freshly ground
black pepper

plenty of finely chopped
fresh **mixed herbs** such
as parsley, chives and
tarragon

1 **shallot**, finely chopped

3 tablespoons **plain flour**

2-3 tablespoons **olive oil**
or basil and garlic oil
(see recipe on page 168)

8-12 soft **goat's cheeses**
such as Chèvretines or 1
log (about 200g/7oz) of
goat's cheese, sliced

4-6 **cherry tomatoes**,
halved

fresh **basil** leaves,
to garnish

Top and tail the courgettes but do not peel them. Grate them finely using a cheese grater or the grating disc of the food processor if you have one.

Put some in a colander and sprinkle with salt. Add more courgettes and salt and continue in this way until they are all used up. Leave in the sink for several hours or until plenty of liquid has drained away.

Press down on the courgettes and/or squeeze them out by handfuls to extract as much liquid as possible – they should be quite dry. Put the eggs, black pepper, chopped herbs, shallot and flour in a bowl and mix together well. Stir in the courgettes.

Heat a little oil in a large, heavy-based frying pan, add the courgette mixture and spread it out evenly in the pan. Fry over a moderate heat until golden brown on the underside.

Put a large plate over the top of the pan and invert the Rösti onto it. Heat a little more oil in the pan, then slide the Rösti back into the pan. Continue cooking until the second side is golden brown and the Rösti is cooked through.

Just before serving, top with goat's cheeses, or slices of goat's cheese, and cherry tomatoes and garnish with basil leaves.

Winter Vegetable Quiche with Yeast Pastry

How to make a wonderful supper dish with the sort of raw materials you might find in a winter organic vegetable box: carrots, parsnips, leeks, celeriac and the odd turnip. The yeast dough gives a nice rustic feel, making this a cross between a quiche and a pizza.

Serves 4

150g (5½oz) **plain flour**

salt and freshly ground black pepper

10g (¼oz) fresh **yeast**, or ½ sachet easy-blend dried yeast

5 tablespoons mixed **milk** and **hot water**

about 500g (1lb 2oz) **mixed root vegetables** (see above for ideas)

a sprig of fresh **thyme**

25g (1oz) **butter**

a squeeze of **lemon juice**

3 **eggs**

100ml (3½fl oz) **whipping cream**

100ml (3½fl oz) plain **fromage frais**

1 tablespoon chopped fresh **chives**

Put the flour, ½ teaspoon salt and the yeast in a food processor and process to work in the yeast. Add the milk and water mixture and process until the mixture forms a ball of dough around the blade. Leave the lid on the processor bowl and allow the dough to rise at room temperature for about 30 minutes.

Preheat the oven to 200°C/400°F/Gas Mark 6. Peel and slice all the vegetables into pieces of roughly equal size. Put 100ml (3½fl oz) water, the thyme and the butter in a wide shallow pan with a lid and bring to a rolling boil.

Add all the vegetables and season with salt and pepper. Cover and cook over a lively heat for 5-6 minutes, until just tender and the water starts to evaporate. Remove the pan from the heat, discard the thyme, stir the lemon juice into the vegetables, then allow them to cool a little.

In a bowl, mix together the eggs, cream, fromage frais and salt and pepper to taste. Stir in the chives. Place a black baking sheet on the lowest oven shelf to get thoroughly hot. Butter a 26cm (10½in) loose-bottomed quiche tin. Knock down the dough, roll it out on a lightly floured surface and use to line the tin. Arrange the vegetables in the bottom of the pastry case and pour the egg mixture over the top.

Place the quiche on the baking sheet in the oven and bake for 20 minutes. Move the quiche (still on its baking sheet) up to the middle shelf and reduce the temperature to 180°C/350°F/Gas Mark 4. Continue baking for a further 15-20 minutes, until the quiche is lightly golden and just set.

Gratin of Courgettes with Mushrooms and Pesto

A robust dish of courgettes layered with mushrooms, pesto, a little cream, and breadcrumbs for the top. The courgettes are best brushed with oil and grilled, rather than fried. This vastly reduces the amount of oil needed.

Put the courgettes in a large colander in layers, sprinkling them with salt as you go. Leave them in the sink to exude some of their juice, and then pat them dry on absorbent kitchen paper.

Preheat the grill to high. Lightly oil a grill pan or baking sheet that will fit under the grill and arrange a layer of courgettes on it. Brush the tops with more oil. Grill the courgettes on one side until flecked with gold, then turn them and grill the second side until lightly browned. Place on a plate and set aside. Repeat with the remaining courgettes.

Preheat the oven to 220°C/425°F/Gas Mark 7. Heat a little oil in a large frying pan and fry the onions until lightly golden. Add the mushrooms, season to taste with salt and pepper, reduce the heat, then cover and cook for 5 minutes until the juices run. Uncover the pan, increase the heat and cook briskly to evaporate the juices, stirring occasionally.

Stir the cream into the pesto. Layer the courgettes, mushroom mixture and pesto cream in an ovenproof dish, finishing with a layer of courgettes and pesto. Sprinkle the breadcrumbs over the top. Bake in the oven for about 20 minutes, or until bubbly and hot and the breadcrumbs are nicely crisp.

Serves 6

1kg (2¼lb) **courgettes**, sliced

salt and freshly ground black pepper

2–3 tablespoons **olive oil**

2 **onions**, sliced

350g (12oz) **mushrooms**, sliced

5 tablespoons **whipping cream**

3 tablespoons **pesto**

3 tablespoons fresh **breadcrumbs**

Crunchy Vegetable Strudel Wrapped in Spinach and Ham

A gorgeous parcel of vegetables rolled up in spinach, cured ham and filo pastry. You can follow the recipe as given or use it as a blueprint for your own personalised parcel, depending on what you have to hand. You need about 600g (1lb 5oz) vegetables, which in spring may include baby carrots, asparagus and spring onions. Later on you could use courgettes, French beans and mangetout. An autumn or winter parcel might contain an assortment of root vegetables such as parsnips, carrots and celeriac. It is important that the vegetables are cooked until crunchy – you can stir-fry (as here), blanch, grill, sauté or roast them, depending on what suits you best. Serve with a bowl of fromage frais, with more fresh herbs snipped in. The strudel is also good cold, although the filo never quite recovers its crispy glory.

Serves 4-6
as a main course or
Serves 8-10
as a starter

6 tablespoons **olive oil**

2 cloves **garlic**, chopped

1 **spring onion**, sliced

1 fresh **red chilli** such as fresno or peperoncini, deseeded and sliced (optional)

200g (7oz) **mushrooms**, sliced or quartered

250g (9oz) **mangetout**, trimmed

200g (7oz) **green asparagus tips**, split in half lengthways

salt and freshly ground black pepper

(continued on opposite page)

Heat 2 tablespoons oil in a wok or large, deep frying pan and briskly stir-fry the garlic, spring onion and chilli, if using, in the oil for a minute or two. Add the mushrooms and stir-fry for another couple of minutes.

Throw in the mangetout and asparagus tips and continue stir-frying for a further 2-3 minutes. Season quite generously with salt and pepper. All the vegetables should be cooked until *al dente*, otherwise you will end up with a soggy mess rather than a crunchy parcel.

Remove the pan from the heat and tip the mixture into a bowl. Stir in the pepper strips, egg, chopped herbs, fromage frais and parmesan. Set aside to cool.

Blanch the chard or spinach leaves in a pan of boiling water, then drain and refresh them in cold water. Pat them dry on a teatowel.

Preheat the oven to 220°C/425°F/Gas Mark 7. Cut a piece (or two, overlapping) of non-stick baking parchment about 50x40cm (20x16in) in size and lay it on your work surface. Arrange the filo pastry sheets in layers on top of the baking parchment to give a rectangle about 45x35cm (17½x14in) in size, brushing each sheet with olive oil as you go. You will need to overlap the sheets slightly to arrive at this size of rectangle. Position the rectangle so that a long edge is nearest you and the short edges are at the sides.

Arrange the chard or spinach leaves on top of the filo sheets to form an inner rectangle and lay the ham slices on top, leaving about a 2.5cm (1in) border all round the edge. Arrange the vegetables so that they cover about half of the surface, along the long edge. Turn the short edges in over the vegetables and roll up the strudel from the long edge closest to you, using the paper to help you. When rolled up, it should be around 10cm (4in) in diameter.

Lift it on its baking parchment onto a baking sheet – preferably one with a lip, as the strudel tends to leak during baking. Brush with more olive oil and sprinkle with seeds if liked. Prepare everything ahead to this point if you wish, and refrigerate the strudel.

Bake the strudel in the oven for 20-25 minutes or until golden brown and crispy. Slice thickly and serve with fromage frais and chopped herbs, if liked.

1 small **red pepper** and 1 small **green pepper**, roasted, skinned, deseeded and cut into strips *(see page 13)*

1 **egg**, lightly beaten

plenty of finely chopped fresh **mixed herbs** in season such as chives, tarragon, parsley and lovage

2-3 tablespoons plain **fromage frais**

1 tablespoon grated **parmesan cheese**

2 large leaves of **Swiss chard** or several leaves of spinach

200g (7oz) packet **filo pastry** sheets

100g (3½oz) thinly sliced **cured ham** such as Black Forest, Westphalian or Prosciutto

sesame, poppy or **pumpkin seeds,** to sprinkle *(optional)*

plain **fromage frais** and chopped fresh **mixed herbs,** to serve *(optional)*

Beetroot, Carrot and Parsnip Terrine

An excellent winter vegetable dish that can be prepared ahead. Be sure to put the beetroot layer at the bottom, otherwise it will seep downwards during the cooking and spoil neighbouring colours. At other times of the year, substitute purées of different seasonal vegetables, making sure you get a good colour contrast.

Serves 6-8

300g (10½oz) cooked, peeled **beetroot**

3 **eggs**

about 150ml (¼ pint) **whipping cream**

salt and freshly ground black pepper

300g (10½oz) cooked **parsnips**

300g (10½oz) cooked **carrots**

Lay a strip of non-stick baking parchment in the bottom of a 25x8x6cm (10x3¼x2½in) or similar size terrine or loaf tin and butter or oil the sides. Set aside. Preheat the oven to 180°C/ 350°F/Gas Mark 4.

Put the beetroot in a blender or food processor with 1 egg, 3 tablespoons cream and salt and pepper to taste, and blend to a smooth purée. Spread it in the bottom of the prepared terrine or tin.

Clean the blender/processor bowl, put in the parsnips with 1 egg, 3 tablespoons cream and salt and pepper to taste, and blend to a smooth purée. Spread this over the beetroot purée.

Once again, clean the blender/processor bowl, put in the carrots with the remaining egg, 3 tablespoons cream and salt and pepper to taste, and blend to a smooth purée. Spread this over the parsnip purée. Cover with a lid or foil and refrigerate if not to be baked immediately.

Put the terrine or loaf tin into a roasting tin and add enough boiling water to come two-thirds of the way up the sides of the terrine. Bake in the oven for about 45 minutes or until the terrine feels firm and springy to the touch.

Remove from the oven and leave for a few minutes before turning out onto a serving dish. Peel away and discard the baking parchment and cut the terrine into slices to serve.

Spring Onion, Courgette, Potato and Bacon Frittata

Frittatas make perfect Sunday evening fare, the ideal dish for using up a bit of this and a little of that, bound together with eggs and a splash of cream. Similar to a Spanish omelette (or a quiche minus the pastry), they are delicious served warm or cold. The trick is not to overdo the cooking, or the frittata will be leathery.

Serves 2

50g (1³/₄oz) **lardons** or **streaky bacon**, *finely chopped*

olive oil or herb oil *(see recipes on page 168), for frying*

2 **spring onions**, *thinly sliced*

1 fresh **green chilli** *such as serrano, jalapeño or peperoncini, deseeded and thinly sliced*

2 small **courgettes**, *diced*

3 *medium* **potatoes**, *boiled, drained and diced*

1 **tomato**, *skinned and chopped*

plenty of chopped fresh **basil**

salt and freshly ground black pepper

4 **eggs**

3 *tablespoons* **single cream**

Put the lardons or bacon in a heavy-based, non-stick frying pan and sweat until the fat runs. Add a little oil if necessary to thinly cover the bottom of the pan. Soften the spring onions and chilli in the oil without allowing them to brown.

Add the courgettes, potatoes, tomato and chopped basil, season to taste with salt and pepper, cover and cook gently until the tomato juices run. Uncover, increase the heat and cook briskly to dry out the mixture, stirring occasionally.

Preheat the grill to high. In a bowl, mix together the eggs, cream and salt and pepper to taste. Pour it into the pan over the bacon and vegetable mixture, stirring to mix.

Cook gently until the frittata is just set around the edges but still creamy in the centre. Watch carefully to ensure that it does not burn on the bottom. When the frittata is just set, put it under the grill briefly until the top is golden brown and puffy.

Rocket Crêpes with Cured Ham and Cream Cheese Filling and Sharp Salsa

Crêpe batter is flavoured with chopped rocket, the resulting cooked crêpes lined with cured ham and filled with low-fat cream cheese. The salsa makes a good counterpoint.

For the batter, put 125ml (4fl oz) water in a blender or food processor with the milk, a pinch of salt, the chopped rocket, flour, eggs and 1 tablespoon herb oil and blend to make a smooth batter. Brush a 20cm (8in) crêpe pan with a little herb oil and make 8 crêpes, following the instructions given in the Fleischschnacka recipe on page 34.

Preheat the oven to 200°C/400°F/Gas Mark 6. For the filling, mix together the cream cheese and fromage frais. Lay slices of cured ham on the crêpes, spread with the cream cheese filling and roll up. Put in an ovenproof dish. Bake in the oven for 10-12 minutes or until lightly golden and the top is crusty.

Meanwhile, make the salsa as instructed on page 111. Garnish the crêpes with rocket leaves and cherry tomatoes and serve the salsa separately.

Serves 4

FOR THE CRÊPES

125ml (4fl oz) **milk**

salt and freshly ground black pepper

a handful of **rocket leaves** (about 25g/1oz), roughly chopped

100g (3½oz) **plain flour**

2 **eggs**

1 tablespoon **herb oil** (see recipes on page 168), plus extra for cooking the crêpes

FOR THE FILLING

250g (9oz) **low-fat cream cheese**

250g (9oz) **plain fromage frais**

200g (7oz) **cured ham** such as Westphalian or Black Forest, very thinly sliced

rocket leaves and halved **cherry tomatoes**, to garnish

sharp salsa (see recipe on page 111)

Tomato and Anchovy Tart 'Tatin'

The idea of baking a tomato tart with the pastry uppermost and then turning it upside-down for serving is a good one, as you avoid the problem of soggy pastry. Choose medium-sized tomatoes for this dish, about 3cm (1¼in) in diameter, such as Gardener's Delight or Sweet 100 rather than the tiny cocktail ones. Serve with a selection of cheeses (especially fresh goat's cheese) and salad.

Serves 2-3

about 500g (1lb 2oz) medium-sized **tomatoes**, halved

salt and freshly ground black pepper

1 tablespoon **olive oil**

a pinch of **caster sugar**

plenty of chopped fresh **mixed herbs** such as basil, oregano and thyme

50g (1¾oz) can **anchovies** in oil, drained

300g (10½oz) ready-made **puff pastry**

fresh **basil** leaves, to garnish

Preheat the oven to 220°C/425°F/Gas Mark 7. Arrange the tomatoes, cut-side down, in a 22cm (8½in) shallow, round ovenproof dish or quiche tin. Pack them in tightly, inclining them slightly so that they all fit. Sprinkle with salt and pepper, oil and sugar, and scatter the chopped herbs on top.

Bake in the oven for 8-10 minutes or until the tomatoes are just cooked. They will exude a lot of juice. Remove from the oven and allow them to cool a bit, then arrange the anchovies on top.

Roll out the pastry on a lightly floured surface to slightly larger than the size of the dish or tin (it will shrink as it bakes). Lay the pastry over the tomatoes and snip the centre with scissors to allow the steam to escape. Bake in the oven for 12-15 minutes or until the pastry is golden.

Remove from the oven and let the tart stand until just before serving, otherwise the juices will seep into the pastry and undo all your good work. Invert a large round plate over it and turn out the tart onto the plate. Garnish with basil leaves.

A Mexican Omelette Stack

Thin omelettes flavoured with herbs and chopped chilli are layered with rajas (chilli and pepper strips) and Prosciutto, and served with tomato salsa for a savoury supper dish.

Serves 2

FOR THE OMELETTES
4 **eggs**
salt and black pepper
1 fresh **green chilli**, deseeded, cut into strips
2 tablespoons chopped fresh **coriander**
olive oil, for frying

FOR THE FILLING
1 **onion**, sliced
1 **red pepper** and 1 **green pepper**, skinned and cut into strips (see page 13)
1-2 fresh **green chilli(es)**, deseeded and cut into strips
6 tablespoons **whipping cream**
5 slices **Prosciutto**

FOR THE SALSA
2 **tomatoes**, quartered
1 small **onion**, chopped
1 fresh **green chilli**, deseeded and chopped
1 tablespoon chopped fresh **coriander**
lemon or **lime juice**

For the omelettes, put the eggs, salt and pepper, chilli, chopped coriander and 1 tablespoon water in a bowl and whisk together to mix. Heat a little oil in a 15cm (6in) heavy-based omelette pan and make 6 thin omelettes in the same way as you would make crêpes, following the instructions in the Fleischschnacka recipe on page 34. Stack up the omelettes on a plate as they are cooked, and set aside.

Preheat the oven to 180°C/350°F/Gas Mark 4. For the filling, heat a little more oil in a frying pan and fry the onion, pepper strips and chilli(es) until soft.

Remove the pan from the heat, season with salt and pepper and stir in 3 tablespoons cream – reserve the remaining cream to spread on top of the omelette stack. Set aside.

Brush a little oil in the base of a deep ovenproof dish the same diameter as the omelettes. Layer these with Prosciutto slices and pepper mixture, finishing with an omelette. Spread the remaining cream on top. Cover with foil.

Bake the omelette stack in the oven for 20-25 minutes or until heated through – stick a skewer in the middle and hold it gingerly to your cheek – it should feel hot, if not, continue cooking for a short while until it is properly hot.

Meanwhile, make the salsa. Put the tomatoes, onion, chilli, coriander and lemon or lime juice, to taste, in a blender or food processor. Blend in short bursts, using the pulse button, so that the salsa retains some texture. Transfer to a small bowl and season to taste with salt and pepper.

Cut the omelette stack into wedges, like a cake, and serve with the cool salsa.

Mushroom and Courgette Burritos
with a Chile Chipotle Salsa

Diced mushrooms and courgettes are tossed in hot oil and bound with a little crème fraîche, wrapped in a flour tortilla, brushed with oil and baked. Chiles chipotles which are used in this recipe, are very hot, smoked chillies, available from speciality shops or by mail order (try The Cool Chile Company, tel 0870 902 1145). The salsa is simplicity itself: stir some chopped chillies into fromage frais. This dish can be prepared ahead and refrigerated until baking time. Serve with Green Chilli Risotto (see recipe on page 73), minus the smoked salmon.

Heat the butter and oil in a large frying pan and soften the shallot and garlic in the pan without allowing them to brown. Add the mushrooms and courgettes, season with salt and pepper, then cover and cook gently for about 5 minutes, until the juices run.

Uncover, increase the heat and cook briskly until the juices have evaporated, stirring occasionally. Remove the pan from the heat, add the chopped coriander and crème fraîche and stir to mix.

If the tortillas are not freshly made, warm them briefly on a griddle (or in a frying pan or in the microwave), just long enough to make them pliable. Divide the mushroom and courgette filling among them, roll up and lay them in an ovenproof baking dish. Cool, cover and chill the filled tortillas if they are not to be baked immediately.

Preheat the oven to 200°C/400°F/Gas Mark 6. Bake the tortillas dry in the oven for about 20 minutes until crispy and hot. Meanwhile, chop the canned chiles finely and stir them into the fromage frais to make the salsa. Serve the hot tortillas with the cold salsa.

Serves 3-4

25g (1oz) **butter**

1 tablespoon **olive oil**

1 **shallot**, finely chopped

1 clove **garlic**, crushed

300g (10½oz) **mushrooms**, finely chopped

300g (10½oz) **courgettes**, finely chopped

salt and freshly ground black pepper

chopped fresh **coriander**, to taste

4 tablespoons **crème fraîche**

six-eight 20cm (8in) diameter **flour tortillas**
(see recipe on page 161)

2 canned **chiles chipotles en adobo**

250ml (9fl oz) plain **fromage frais**

Polenta Layered with Leeks and a Blue Cheese Sauce with Walnuts

If you're looking for a robust supper dish for autumn or winter, this is the one: polenta is cooked, cooled, sliced and layered with a blue cheese sauce and crunchy cooked leeks. The walnut topping provides a good contrast.

Serves 3-4

FOR THE POLENTA

125g (4½oz) quick-cook **polenta**

300ml (½pint) **milk**

salt and freshly ground black pepper

FOR THE LEEKS AND CHEESE SAUCE

2-3 **leeks**, about 300g (10½oz) in weight, washed and thickly sliced

40g (1½oz) **butter**

1 heaped tablespoon **plain flour**

325ml (11fl oz) **milk**

1 **bay leaf**

75g (2¾oz) **blue cheese** such as stilton or gorgonzola

2 tablespoons chopped **walnuts**

plenty of chopped fresh flat-leaf **parsley**, to garnish

Make the polenta in a saucepan, as instructed on the packet, mixing it with the milk, 200ml (7fl oz) water and 1 teaspoon salt. Tip it into a shallow rectangular dish or an empty rectangular ice cream carton; alternatively tip it onto a wooden board and shape it into a rectangle about 4cm (1½in) deep. Allow it to cool until quite firm.

Lightly grease a shallow ovenproof dish and set aside. Preheat the oven to 200°C/400°F/Gas Mark 6. Put the leeks in a shallow pan with 15g (½oz) butter, salt and pepper and 3 tablespoons water. Bring to the boil, cover and cook briskly for 8-10 minutes or until the water has evaporated and the leeks are stewing in their own juices, stirring once or twice.

Meanwhile, for the sauce, melt the remaining butter in a saucepan and stir in the flour. Stir in the milk, add the bay leaf, then bring to the boil, stirring. Simmer for 5 minutes, then remove and discard the bay leaf and crumble in the blue cheese. Season to taste with salt and pepper.

Slice the cooled polenta vertically into 1cm (½in) thick slices, then cut into triangles. Place half the triangles in the prepared dish. Cover with half the cheese sauce and all the leeks. Top with the remaining triangles and pour the remaining cheese sauce over the polenta. Sprinkle the walnuts on top.

Bake in the oven for 20-30 minutes or until golden brown and bubbly. Sprinkle with chopped parsley to garnish, just before serving.

Polenta with Ham and Piperade

An excellent supper dish, good for using up the end bits from a ham or piece of gammon. These are sandwiched between layers of piperade, with herby polenta under and over.

Serves 4-6

2 tablespoons **olive oil**

2 **shallots**, thinly sliced

2 cloves **garlic**, crushed

1 **pepper**, any colour, deseeded and cut into strips

salt and freshly ground black pepper

800g (1¾lb) can or two 400g (14oz) cans **tomatoes** with their juice

2 good pinches of dried **oregano**

a splash of **Tabasco sauce**

250g (9oz) quick-cook **polenta**

400ml (14fl oz) **ham** or **gammon stock**

600ml (1 pint) **milk**

1-2 tablespoons chopped fresh **mixed herbs** such as parsley, chives and oregano

about 200g (7oz) **cooked ham** or gammon, cut into strips

plain **fromage frais**, to serve

Preheat the oven to 200°C/400°F/Gas Mark 6. Heat the oil gently in a large frying pan and soften the shallots and garlic in the oil without allowing them to brown. Add the pepper strips, season to taste with salt and pepper, then cover and cook gently for about 10 minutes, or until the peppers are a little soft.

Stir in the tomatoes, oregano and Tabasco sauce, cover and cook gently for a further 5 minutes. Uncover, increase the heat and cook, stirring, until the mixture is somewhat reduced. Check and adjust the seasoning.

Make the polenta in a saucepan, as instructed on the packet, mixing it with the stock, milk and salt and pepper to taste (if you have used ham stock, go easy on the salt). Cook, stirring vigorously – it will plop about alarmingly – for about 5 minutes or until thickened. Stir in the chopped herbs, then remove the pan from the heat.

Spread half the polenta in an ovenproof dish, top with half the pepper mixture, and arrange the ham or gammon strips on top. Top with the rest of the pepper mixture and the remaining polenta.

Bake in the oven for 30-40 minutes or until hot throughout – test by sticking a skewer into the centre and holding it gingerly against your cheek. If it is not thoroughly hot, continue cooking for a short while. Serve with the fromage frais alongside. Serve with salad.

Potato Gratin with Lemon and Shallots

Vegetable dishes that can be prepared ahead are worth their weight in gold. Here is an excellent one that has a particular affinity with duck or chicken: a rich mash flavoured with chopped lemon and shallots.

Peel the potatoes and cook them in a pan of boiling, salted water with the whole lemon until both are tender. Drain, reserve the lemon and mash the potatoes with 25g (1oz) butter and the egg yolks. Set aside.

Halve the lemon and pick out and discard the pips. Cut the flesh and skin into little dice and set aside.

Preheat the oven to 200°C/400°F/Gas Mark 6. Melt 25g (1oz) butter in a pan and soften the shallots in the butter until pale golden. Increase the heat, add the diced lemon and cook briskly for a few minutes, stirring occasionally. Remove the pan from the heat and stir the lemon mixture into the mashed potatoes.

Brush an ovenproof dish lightly with oil and tip in the potato mixture. Cut the remaining butter into cubes and scatter over the top. The dish can be prepared ahead up to this point, cooled and refrigerated.

Bake the potato gratin in the oven for 20-25 minutes or until golden and crusty.

Serves 4-6

750g (1lb 10oz) floury **potatoes**

salt

1 **lemon**, scrubbed

75g (2³⁄₄oz) **butter**

2 **egg yolks**

2 **shallots**, finely chopped

Potato, Bacon and Munster Pasties

A sort of Alsace version of Cornish pasties: instead of meat and potatoes, the filling is of sliced Munster cheese, diced bacon and potatoes. They are quite outrageously calorific – and utterly delicious. Serve with mixed salad leaves.

Makes 6 pasties

200g (7oz) **lardons** or **streaky bacon**, finely chopped

400g (14oz) firm, waxy **potatoes** or new potatoes

salt

200g (7oz) **Munster cheese** or camembert

600g (1lb 5oz) ready-made **puff pastry**

1 **egg**, beaten, to glaze

caraway seeds, to sprinkle

Line a baking sheet with non-stick baking parchment and set aside. Sweat the lardons or bacon in a small, heavy-based frying pan without extra fat, until the fat runs. Do not let them get more than lightly golden, or they will toughen. Lift them out with a slotted spoon and drain on absorbent kitchen paper. Set aside.

Meanwhile, cook the potatoes in a pan of boiling, salted water for about 15 minutes or until barely tender. Drain, cool slightly, then peel and dice the potatoes and set aside. Pare the rind away from the circumference of the cheese but leave on the top and bottom rinds. Slice the cheese into 12 slices and set aside.

Preheat the oven to 200°C/400°F/Gas Mark 6. Cut the pastry into 6 equal-sized pieces. Roll out each piece of pastry on a lightly floured surface to a roughly circular shape. Using a plate 20cm (8in) in diameter, trim each piece of pastry to a 20cm (8in) circle. Put a slice of cheese on one half of the pastry disc, add some bacon pieces and potatoes, then top with another slice of cheese.

Wet a border around half the circumference of the pastry, close up and press the edges together to give a pasty or turnover. Crimp the edges together or press them with a fork to give a decorative finish.

Put them onto the prepared baking sheet and brush all over with beaten egg. Sprinkle with caraway seeds. Chill until required, if liked. Bake the pasties in the oven for 15-20 minutes or until the pastry is golden brown.

Chard Parcels with Polenta, Chillies and Cheese in a Tomato Sauce

A Mexican-inspired vegetable dish rather reminiscent of tamales (though much lighter): blanched chard leaves are wrapped around a filling of polenta, cheese and chilli and served with a spicy, creamy tomato sauce (spinach can be used in place of chard, though it is hard to find leaves big enough). The dish can be prepared entirely in advance.

Lightly oil an ovenproof dish and set aside. Cut the chard leaves from the stems and chop the stems into small cubes.

Bring a large pan of salted water to the boil and blanch the leaves briefly, one by one, in the boiling water. Lift them out with a fish slice, refresh in a sink of cold water and drain them on a teatowel. In the same water, cook the stems for 2-3 minutes or until just tender, then drain. Set aside.

Make the polenta in a saucepan, as instructed on the packet, mixing it with the milk, 300ml (½ pint) water and salt and pepper. Remove the pan from the heat and stir in the chard stalks, cheese and one of the chopped chillies. Divide the mixture evenly between the chard leaves, then roll and fold them into parcels. Place them seam-side down in the prepared ovenproof dish and set aside.

Put the tomatoes, garlic, onion, remaining chilli and salt and pepper to taste in a blender or food processor and blend until smooth. Heat the oil in a frying pan and fry the tomato sauce for about 5 minutes, stirring, until it is thick.

Preheat the oven to 200°C/400°F/Gas Mark 6. Remove the pan from the heat and whisk in the cream. Check and adjust the seasoning. Pour the sauce over the parcels. Cool and refrigerate if the dish is to be baked later.

Bake the parcels in the oven for 20-30 minutes, until thoroughly hot and bubbly.

Serves 4-6

8 chard leaves, about 25x20cm (10x8in) in size, with stems

salt and freshly ground black pepper

125g (4½oz) medium-fine quick-cook **polenta**

300ml (½ pint) **milk**

100g (3½oz) **cheddar cheese**, diced

2 fresh **red chillies** such as fresno or peperoncini, deseeded and finely chopped

400g (14oz) can **tomatoes** with their juice

1 clove **garlic**, crushed

1 **onion**, finely chopped

1 tablespoon **olive oil**

4 tablespoons **whipping cream**

Yorkshire Puddings Filled with Ceps and/or Mushrooms and Bacon

An excellent supper dish, or a starter. If you prefer, you can buy ready-made Yorkshire puddings – the filling is enough for about eight. If you can't find ceps in your neck of the woods, use all cultivated mushrooms instead.

Serves 4-8, *depending on your menu*

FOR THE YORKSHIRE PUDDINGS

125ml (4fl oz) mixed **milk** and **water** (half and half)

50g (1¾oz) **plain flour**

2 tablespoons **olive oil**

2 **eggs**

salt and freshly ground black pepper

FOR THE FILLING

100g (3½oz) **lardons** or **streaky bacon**, finely chopped

12g (¼oz) **butter**

250g (9oz) cultivated **mushrooms**, quartered

200g (7oz) **ceps**, cut the same size as the above

2-3 tablespoons **crème fraîche**

For the Yorkshire puddings, put the milk and water, flour, 1 tablespoon oil, eggs and a pinch of salt in a blender or food processor and blend until smooth. Scrape down the sides and blend again. Pour into a bowl, cover and refrigerate for an hour or two.

Preheat the oven to 220°C/425°F/Gas Mark 7. Put a drop of the remaining oil into each hole of an 8-hole muffin tin and put it in the oven to get thoroughly hot. Pour the batter into the muffin tin dividing it evenly between each hole. Bake in the oven for 12-15 minutes or until well-risen, golden brown and billowy. Run a knife round the edge of each one, turn them out onto a wire rack and set aside. Lower the oven temperature to 200°C/400°F/Gas Mark 6.

Meanwhile, for the filling, put the lardons or bacon in a frying pan; sweat them gently until the fat runs and they are lightly golden. Add the butter, then stir in the mushrooms, ceps and seasoning. Cover and cook gently for 5 minutes.

Uncover, increase the heat and cook briskly for a further 5-6 minutes, or until the juices evaporate, stirring occasionally. Stir in the crème fraîche and cook briefly to bind.

Invert the baked Yorkshire puddings (as they cook, they billow up into a dome; underneath is a hole, which will now be filled) and place them in ramekin dishes. Fill each one with the mushroom mixture.

Bake the filled Yorkshire puddings in the oven for 10-12 minutes or until thoroughly hot and a little bubbly on top.

Mixed Mushrooms En Croute with Tarragon

You can use any number of different mushrooms, wild and/or cultivated, for this delicious dish. It makes a great starter, or a main course served with salad. Prepare the dish ahead of time, glaze with most of the beaten egg to stop the pastry drying out and refrigerate it. Just before baking, glaze with more egg and sprinkle with sesame seeds.

Line a heavy baking sheet with non-stick baking parchment and set aside. Heat the oil in a pan and sweat the shallot and garlic gently in the oil without allowing them to brown. Stir in the mushrooms and salt and pepper to taste. Cover and cook gently for 5-10 minutes or until the juices run. Preheat the oven to 220°C/425°F/Gas Mark 7.

Uncover the pan of mushrooms, increase the heat and cook briskly to evaporate the juices, stirring occasionally. Remove the pan from the heat, stir in the chopped tarragon and crème fraîche and set aside to cool. Roll out the pastry on a well-floured board to a rectangle about 35x45cm (14x17½in) in size. Position the rectangle so that a long edge is nearest you. Sprinkle the breadcrumbs all over the surface of the pastry almost to the edges. Spread the mushrooms in a rectangle so that they cover about half of the surface, along the long edge. Brush the outside edges with water and roll up from the long edge like a Swiss roll. Press the ends together to seal.

Place it on the prepared baking sheet – if it is a bit long for the baking sheet, either lay it diagonally or curl it up like a horseshoe. Brush with a little beaten egg and refrigerate if not to be baked immediately. Just before baking, brush with the remaining beaten egg and sprinkle with sesame seeds.

Bake in the oven for 30-35 minutes or until golden brown and cooked through. Slice and serve with the fromage frais and tarragon, if liked.

*Serves 4-6
as a light main course or
Serves 8-10 as a starter*

1 tablespoon **olive oil**

1 **shallot**, finely chopped

1 clove **garlic**, crushed

500g (1lb 2oz) mixed **mushrooms**, quartered or sliced depending on size

salt and freshly ground black pepper

plenty of finely chopped fresh **tarragon**

3 tablespoons **crème fraîche**

300g (10½oz) ready-made **puff pastry**

25g (1oz) fresh **breadcrumbs** (about 4 tablespoons)

1 **egg**, beaten

2 tablespoons **sesame seeds**

a bowl of plain **fromage frais** mixed with some chopped fresh **tarragon**, to serve (optional)

For most people, rice is hugely important – it is the main foodstuff for over half the world's population. For all practical purposes, it falls broadly into two categories: long-grain or Indian rice (*Oryza indica*) and short-grain or Japanese rice (*Oryza japonica*). Long-grain in its various manifestations (Patna, Carolina, Basmati, Surinam, Thai, Jasmine) is the one to use for pilaffs or other dishes where you want autonomous grains. Short-grain (Arborio, Carnaroli, Vialone) is right for creamy risottos because the particular nature of its starch content means it will stick together nicely when cooked, while still retaining its firmness.

Most rice is refined and therefore white. Brown rice (sometimes called wholegrain) can be either long- or short-grain and is unrefined, retaining much of its natural nutritional value. Other varieties, such as red rice (*Oryza glaberrima*) and wild rice (*Ziziana aquatica*) are best mixed with the conventional varieties – partly because they are rather chewy and assertive, but also because they are expensive and a little goes a long way.

Rice lends itself to almost endless variations and is one of the best fast foods I know. Here are a number of tasty ideas featuring different types of rice and flavourings. Most are interesting enough to stand on their own, or they can be used to accompany plainly cooked or grilled meat, poultry or fish. Most rice dishes can be prepared in advance, left to cool thoroughly and then reheated (covered) either in a moderate oven or microwave.

Tomato Pilaff with Bacon and Avocado

This makes an excellent supper dish, or would go well with roast or grilled meat or fish. The crispy bacon bits provide a good crunchy contrast to the rice and avocado.

Serves 4

100g (3½oz) **lardons** or **streaky bacon**, *finely chopped*

1 tablespoon **olive oil**

1 **shallot**, *finely chopped*

1 clove **garlic**, *crushed*

250g (9oz) **long-grain rice**

2 **tomatoes**, *skinned, deseeded and chopped*

500ml (18fl oz) **vegetable stock**

salt and freshly ground black pepper

1 **avocado**, *peeled, stoned and cut into cubes*

In a small, heavy-based saucepan or casserole dish, fry the lardons or bacon in the oil until lightly golden and crispy. Lift them out with a slotted spoon and drain on absorbent kitchen paper. Set aside.

Soften the shallot and garlic in the same pan without allowing them to brown. Stir in the rice and fry briskly for a few minutes, stirring continuously. Add the tomato flesh and stir over a moderate heat for a few minutes more, until the tomatoes have dried out a little.

Pour in the stock, add salt and pepper to taste, cover and cook for 15-16 minutes. Lift the lid and taste the rice. The stock should all be absorbed and the rice should be just *al dente*.

Just before serving, fork in the avocado cubes and reserved lardons or bacon.

Vegetable Paella

Here's a nice version of vegetable paella, using a mixture of vegetables and long-grain rice. For vegetables use the recipe as a guide, substituting whatever is in season – you need a total of 600g (1lb 5oz). Slice them or cut them into strips, making sure you cut them all to about the same size.

Heat the oil in a large shallow pan and soften the onion, garlic, pepper and chilli in the oil. Increase the heat, add the tomatoes and cook, stirring, for 5-6 minutes to dry the mixture out a bit.

Stir in the rice and cook for a further 5-6 minutes, stirring occasionally. Dissolve the saffron in the boiling stock. Add 800ml (28fl oz) of the stock to the pan, then stir in the prepared vegetables. Season to taste with salt and pepper, cover the pan, reduce the heat to moderate and cook for 15 minutes.

Lift the lid and taste the rice – it should be just *al dente* and the stock absorbed. If there is still stock floating about, do not add the rest but cook the rice for a further 5 minutes to dry it out. If the stock is all absorbed and the rice is not quite cooked, add the remaining stock and cook for a further 5 minutes. Serve, garnished with sprigs of thyme on top.

Serves 6

2 tablespoons **olive oil**

1 **onion**, finely chopped

1 clove **garlic**, crushed

1 **pepper**, deseeded and cut into strips

1 **red chilli**, deseeded and finely chopped

2 **tomatoes**, skinned, deseeded and chopped

400g (14oz) **long-grain rice**

2 pinches **saffron** threads

800ml-1 litre (1½-1¾ pints) boiling **vegetable** or **chicken stock**

150g (5½oz) **fennel**, chopped

150g (5½oz) **courgettes**, chopped

150g (5½oz) **leeks**, washed and sliced

150g (5½oz) **carrots**, chopped

salt and freshly ground black pepper

sprigs of fresh **thyme**

Kashmir Rice with Gingered Prawns, Lemon Grass and Coconut Milk

A lovely dish with subtle flavours and textures. Any interesting long-grain rice can be substituted for kashmir (jasmine, Thai or basmati, for instance).

Serves 6

2 tablespoons **olive oil**

500g (1lb 2oz) raw, unshelled **prawns**

a walnut-sized piece of **fresh root ginger**, peeled and grated

salt and freshly ground black pepper

4 stalks **lemon grass**, trimmed and sliced on a slant

2 fresh **green chillies** such as serrano, jalapeño or peperoncini, deseeded and finely chopped

350g (12oz) **kashmir rice**

400g (14oz) can unsweetened **coconut milk**

a small bunch of **spring onions** (3-4), trimmed and sliced

juice of 2 **limes**

Heat the oil in a large, heavy-based pan, add the prawns, ginger and salt and pepper to taste and fry until the prawns have turned pink. Remove the prawns from the pan, place on a plate and keep hot.

Add the lemon grass, chillies and rice to the pan and fry, stirring, for 5-6 minutes. Add 350ml (12fl oz) water, the coconut milk and salt to taste. Cover and cook for 15 minutes or until the rice is *al dente* and holes start to appear on the surface.

Remove the pan from the heat, fork half the spring onions into the rice, lay the cooked prawns on top and sprinkle with lime juice. Let the dish stand, covered, for 5 minutes. Sprinkle the remaining spring onions on top and serve.

Risotto with Dried Ceps and Chipotle Chiles

*H*ere is a wonderful, Mexican-Italian risotto for a winter evening. Chipotles (obtainable from specialist Mexican shops) are to the chilli family as Lapsang Souchong is to tea – they have the same sort of smoky complexity of flavour, plus a tremendous kick. They also seem to have a pleasing affinity with dried ceps. Serve the risotto as a main dish with soured cream or fromage frais, or use it to accompany barbecued or roasted meat or fish. If you like your food spicy, puncture the chiles with a skewer while the risotto is cooking; otherwise leave them whole, in which case they will infuse the rice with a gentle smoky heat. Remove them before serving.

Serves 2-3

2-3 dried
chiles chipotles

25-50g (1-1¾oz)
dried ceps

2 tablespoons **olive oil**

1 **onion**, finely chopped

1 clove **garlic**, crushed

200g (7oz) **short-grain rice** such as arborio

1 **chicken** or **vegetable stock cube**, crumbled

salt

soured cream, to serve

Put the chiles chipotles and the ceps in a bowl and cover with 1 litre (1¾ pints) hot water. Leave them for about 1 hour or until a little softened. Drain the chiles and mushrooms, reserving the soaking water and chiles and mushrooms separately. Strain the soaking water into a bowl through muslin or a nappy liner.

Heat the oil in a heavy-based pan and soften the onion and garlic in the oil without allowing them to brown. Stir in the rice and fry for 5-10 minutes or until glistening and glazed-looking. Stir in the drained chiles and ceps and the crumbled stock cube.

Measure out 800ml (28fl oz) of the reserved soaking water. Add it to the risotto in 200ml (7fl oz) doses, each time allowing the liquid to evaporate. Keep stirring, tasting and seasoning carefully with salt if needed as you cook. You may not need all the liquid – I find that something between 600ml and 800ml (20fl oz and 28fl oz) of liquid is about right. Aim to arrive at a result where the liquid is absorbed and the rice is just *al dente* but still a little soupy.

Just before serving, remove and discard the chiles and put a blob of soured cream on top of each serving.

Green Chilli Risotto with Smoked Salmon

A tasty and exceedingly pretty dish: risotto flecked with fresh green chillies and pale pink smoked salmon. Serve with a bowl of low-fat fromage frais.

Heat the oil in a heavy-based pan and soften the onion in the oil without allowing it to brown. Add the chillies and rice and fry for a few minutes, stirring, until the rice is glistening.

Add 750ml (26fl oz) of the hot stock, season to taste with salt and pepper and cook for 15-16 minutes, stirring from time to time, until the rice is *al dente* but still a little soupy. Stir in the remaining stock if needed and continue cooking until done.

Fork in the smoked salmon and serve at once in soup bowls. Garnish with chervil sprigs at the last minute.

Serves 2-3
as a main course

2 tablespoons **olive oil**

1 **onion**, finely chopped

2-3 fresh **green chillies** such as serrano, jalapeño or peperoncini, deseeded and cut into strips

250g (9oz) **short-grain rice** such as arborio

about 1 litre (1¾ pints) **vegetable** or **chicken stock**

salt and freshly ground black pepper

100g (3½oz) **smoked salmon**, diced

fresh **chervil** sprigs, to garnish

Lemon Risotto with Scallops and Rosemary

I love this recipe with its clean, sharp, lemony flavour offset by the sweetness of the scallops (or prawns, if you prefer), and a scattering of sliced spring onions on top. Wonderful for a rather classy kitchen supper, or a first course before a simply grilled meat or fish dish. The smell of rosemary, released by the heat of the risotto, is intensely delicious.

Heat 2 tablespoons oil in a pan and soften the onion and garlic in the oil without allowing them to brown. Stir in the rice and continue to cook for a few minutes, stirring, until the rice is glistening.

Add the lemon juice, salt and pepper and about a cupful of stock. Cook briskly, stirring, until it is absorbed. Add another cupful of stock and repeat the procedure until all the stock is used up and the rice is tender and creamy.

Dust the scallops in seasoned flour. Heat the remaining oil in a frying pan and fry the scallops very briefly until lightly golden, turning once – this will only take 2-3 minutes.

Divide the risotto among warmed soup bowls, arrange the scallops on top, sprinkle with spring onions and garnish with rosemary sprigs.

Serves 3-4

3 tablespoons **olive oil**

1 **onion**, finely chopped

1 clove **garlic**, crushed

300g (10½oz) **short-grain rice** such as arborio

juice of 2 **lemons**

salt and freshly ground black pepper

about 1.2 litres (2 pints) **fish** or **vegetable stock**

12-15 fresh shelled **scallops**, trimmed of muscle

seasoned **plain flour**, for dusting

3 **spring onions**, thinly sliced

fresh **rosemary** sprigs, to garnish

Next to bread-making, producing home-made pasta is one of the most creative and satisfying of kitchen activities – and it's much easier than you might think. All you need is a big bowl (or food processor) for mixing, a rolling pin and good tummy and arm muscles for rolling out, and a sharp knife to cut the pasta to the required shape.

You can live without a pasta machine – in fact rolling out by hand has the advantage of giving a decent-sized sheet from which to cut custom-sized ravioli, cannelloni, lasagne or other pasta, rather than the 10cm (4in) wide strips dictated by hand-cranked pasta machines. Noodles are also just as easily cut by hand from the rolled out pasta sheets: roll them up roulade-style and cut to the required width. (And, of course, nowadays fresh pasta is readily available in many shops and makes a wonderfully quick meal with a simple sauce and salad.)

Although the best commercial dried pasta is made from durum wheat flour, this is rarely available in shops. For home-made pasta, a strong white bread flour (*Type 55* in France), which has a good gluten content, works very well. Thereafter the only ingredients are salt, eggs (roughly 1 per 100g/3½ oz flour) and a splash of oil.

I like to mix influences in pasta dishes, serving them with spicy Mexican salsas, or robust Swiss-type onion sauces. The filled pastas are more of a production, definitely for those who like playing with their food – if your kitchen is big enough and you can muster a bunch of like-minded friends, throw a pasta party and have everyone come and help. Many hands are needed, between rolling out, cutting, filling and sauces, and there's the shared complicity of a meal in which everyone has had a hand.

PASTA
possibilities

Dough for Fresh Pasta

Makes about 500g (1lb 2oz) pasta dough, *for ravioli, lasagne, cannelloni, noodles etc, enough to* **serve 6–8** *as a starter or to* **serve 4–6** *as a main course*

3 large **eggs**

1 teaspoon salt

1 tablespoon **olive oil**

250–300g (9–10½oz) **strong white bread flour**

To make dough in the food processor: put in the eggs, salt and oil and process until well mixed. With the motor running, add 250g (9oz) flour in a steady stream and process until the dough comes together in a ball and cleans itself off the sides of the bowl. If the dough is still very sticky, add more flour. Continue processing until well kneaded. The dough should be firm and smooth, and not at all sticky. Wrap in cling wrap and leave to rest for at least 1 hour.

To make dough by hand: put 250g (9oz) flour and salt in a bowl and make a well in the centre. Mix together the eggs and oil and put them into the well. Mix in the flour and work up to a firm, smooth dough. If the dough is still very sticky, add more flour. Turn out onto a board and knead very thoroughly until firm, smooth and not at all sticky to the hands. Wrap in cling wrap and leave to rest for at least 1 hour.

To roll and cut pasta by hand: cut the pasta dough in half and roll out each piece very thinly to a large rectangle about the size of a teatowel. For ribbon noodles (tagliatelle etc.), roll the dough up like a Swiss roll and cut to the desired width. Dust liberally with flour, shake them out and leave on a cool surface to dry out a bit. Alternatively, cut ravioli, cannelloni or lasagne of the size you wish.

If using a hand-cranked pasta machine: cut the dough into 6 equal-sized pieces. Roll out each piece starting on the widest setting. Decrease the setting by 2 steps each time until you are on the finest setting. You may need to cut the pasta sheets in half, otherwise they will get very long. For noodles, insert the handle in the noodle cutting blade and feed the sheets through. Shake them out and put them on a lavishly floured board. If the cutters don't go right through the pasta sheet, let it dry out a little more. Leave it to rest at room temperature.

Pepper Pasta Fresca

A gorgeously gaudy dish of home-made (or dried red, white and green) ribbon noodles, strips of yellow peppers, green beans, nasturtium or pot marigold flowers (if you can lay hands on them) and toasted poppy seeds, bathed in a red pepper sauce, lightly spiked with chilli.

Roast or grill the peppers as instructed on page 13. Skin and deseed them, then cut the flesh into strips. Set the yellow pepper strips aside. Put the red pepper strips in a blender or food processor with the cream, salt and chilli powder and blend until smooth. Set this sauce aside.

Cook the noodles in a large pan of boiling, salted water for 2-3 minutes, until just tender, or according to the packet instructions. Drain well and return the noodles to the pan with the yellow pepper strips, beans and red pepper sauce and toss to mix. Check and adjust the seasoning, if necessary.

Put the poppy seeds in a small heavy-based pan without any fat and heat them gently until they smell fragrant.

Serve the pasta on warmed plates and sprinkle with poppy seeds. Garnish with the flowers, if using.

Serves 4

1 **yellow pepper**

1 **red pepper**

100ml (3½fl oz) **whipping cream**

salt, to taste

1 teaspoon **chilli powder**

1 quantity **fresh pasta dough** cut into fine noodles
(see recipe on opposite page)
or 250g (9oz) dried mixed coloured ribbon noodles (e.g. red, green and white)

100g (3½oz) **French beans**, trimmed and lightly cooked

1 tablespoon **poppy seeds**

nasturtium flowers or pot marigold (calendula) flowers, to garnish (optional)

Tagliatelle with a Salsa of Dried Chillies and Tomato

Guajillo chiles – dark brick-red, smooth and shiny – pack a powerful punch. In this smooth sauce of guajillos and tomatoes, the chiles are tamed with a little cream. Any of the other dried Mexican chillies (pasilla, ancho, chipotle) could be substituted to good effect. The resulting sauce provides a good foil to pasta, and goes beautifully with grilled chicken or fish.

Serves 6 *as a starter* or **Serves 4** *as a main course*

4-5 **chiles guajillos** or other Mexican dried chillies

1 small **onion**

2 cloves **garlic**

2cm (¾in) piece of **cinnamon stick**

400g (14oz) can **tomatoes** with their juice

salt and freshly ground black pepper

a pinch of **caster sugar**

olive oil, for frying

100ml (3½fl oz) **single cream**

(continued on opposite page)

Cut the stalks off the chiles, slit them open and remove and discard the seeds. Peel the onion and cut it in half; leave the garlic unpeeled. Heat an ungreased heavy-based frying pan or a griddle over a moderate heat.

Put the chiles, onion halves and garlic in the pan or on the griddle and cook to toast them gently. After about 5 minutes, the chiles should become supple and aromatic – they must not burn, or the sauce will be bitter. Flatten them with a spatula as they are toasting, and turn them occasionally. Let the onion and garlic get slightly browned.

Remove the pan from the heat, lift the chiles out of the pan into a bowl and cover them with hot water. Leave for about 15 minutes or until soft. Slip the garlic out of its skin, then put the garlic in a blender or food processor with the onion and cinnamon.

When the chiles are soft, drain them, then add them to the blender with the tomatoes. Blend until smooth and well mixed, then season to taste with salt and pepper and add the sugar. Push the tomato mixture through a sieve and discard the residue.

Heat a little oil in a deep, heavy-based pan, add the tomato sauce and fry for about 10 minutes, or until the sauce is thick and syrupy, stirring occasionally. Check and adjust the seasoning. Stir in 250ml (9fl oz) water to make it into a lightly coating consistency and bring it briefly back to the boil. Remove the pan from the heat and whisk in the single cream.

Meanwhile, cook the noodles, tagliatelle or linguine in a large pan of boiling, salted water until just tender, or according to the packet instructions. Drain well, then add the tagliatelle to the tomato sauce, tossing to coat well.

Serve in soup bowls with a dollop of yoghurt on top of each portion. Serve the chopped coriander and spring onions separately for everyone to sprinkle over the pasta al gusto.

1 quantity **fresh pasta dough** (see recipe on page 78) cut into fine noodles or 300g (10½oz) dried tagliatelle or linguine

natural **yoghurt**, to serve

plenty of chopped fresh **coriander** and **spring onions**, to serve

Lasagne de la Mer

A sensational dish for spring: lasagne layered with thinly sliced salmon and white fish with a vivid green sauce. If you can't find (or don't like) wild garlic, substitute spinach. And if you can't be bothered with making your own pasta dough, substitute bought lasagne. It's a practical dish for a supper party, as the whole thing can be prepared ahead, ready for baking.

Serves 8 generously as a main course

1 quantity **fresh pasta dough** *(see recipe on page 78)* or 300g (10½oz) dried lasagne

25g (1oz) **butter**

a good handful of **wild garlic leaves** or **fresh spinach leaves** *(about 100g/3½oz)*, shredded

1 tablespoon **plain flour**

250ml (9fl oz) **fish** or **vegetable stock**

125ml (4fl oz) **whipping cream**

salt and freshly ground black pepper

500-600g (1lb 2oz-1lb 5oz) skinless, boneless **salmon fillet**

500-600g (1lb 2oz-1lb 5oz) skinless, boneless **white fish fillet** such as haddock

Roll out the fresh pasta dough very thinly and cut into lasagne sheets to fit the chosen baking dish (about 30x35cm/12x14in is a good size). Lightly oil the dish and set aside. Blanch the bought lasagne in a large pan of boiling, salted water until limp. Drain, refresh and leave in cold water until required.

For the sauce, melt the butter in a heavy-based pan and soften the wild garlic leaves or spinach in the butter until just wilted. Stir in the flour and cook for a couple of minutes. Stir in the stock, cream and salt and pepper to taste, bring to the boil, stirring, then simmer for 10 minutes, stirring occasionally.

Preheat the oven to 200°C/400°F/Gas Mark 6. Remove the pan from the heat, cool slightly then put the mixture in a blender or food processor (or leave in the pan and use a hand-held blender) and blend until smooth. Set aside.

Cut the fish into thin slices horizontally and season lightly with salt and pepper. Spread a little sauce in the bottom of the prepared baking dish, lay some lasagne on top and arrange some fish pieces over the lasagne. Add more sauce, lasagne and fish until all are used up, finishing with a layer of pasta topped with some sauce. The dish can be prepared ahead up to this point, cooled, covered and refrigerated.

Bake the lasagne in the oven for 15-20 minutes or until thoroughly hot. Stick a skewer in the middle to test – it should feel quite warm if held gingerly to the cheek. Serve immediately.

Vegetable Lasagne à la Mexicana

*H*ere's a Mexican-type lasagne in which a smooth tomato sauce replaces béchamel and the layers are of courgettes, sweetcorn, peppers, chillies and fromage frais.

Brush an ovenproof dish lightly with oil and set aside. For the tomato sauce, finely chop 1 onion. Heat 1 tablespoon oil in a saucepan and soften the onion and 1 clove garlic gently in the oil. Add the tomatoes, mashing them with a potato masher, then add the sugar. Season to taste with salt and pepper. Simmer the sauce for 20 minutes or until well seasoned and slightly thickened, stirring occasionally.

Meanwhile, if using dried pasta, blanch the lasagne for 5 minutes in a large pan of boiling, salted water until just limp. Drain and leave to soak in cold water so that the sheets do not stick together. Chop the remaining 2 onions.

Heat 1 tablespoon oil in a heavy-based pan and soften the chopped onions and remaining garlic in the oil without allowing them to brown. Add the peppers and chillies and fry for about 5 minutes or until just softened, stirring.

Scrape this mixture into a bowl and set it aside. Add the remaining oil to the pan and fry the courgette strips briskly until lightly golden, turning them once. Remove the pan from the heat and set aside.

Preheat the oven to 200°C/400°F/Gas Mark 6. Spoon some tomato sauce into the prepared dish and add a layer of lasagne. Follow with some pepper mixture, courgettes, sweetcorn, fromage frais and more tomato sauce. Season. Repeat the layers, finishing with lasagne topped with tomato sauce, then fromage frais and parmesan cheese. If not to be baked immediately, cool, cover and chill the dish.

Bake the lasagne in the oven for 20-25 minutes or until thoroughly hot and bubbly.

Serves 6-8

3 onions

3 tablespoons **olive oil**

2 cloves **garlic**, crushed

800g (1¾lb) can or two 400g (14oz) cans **tomatoes** with their juice

a pinch of **caster sugar**

salt and freshly ground black pepper

½ quantity **fresh pasta dough** (see recipe on page 78), cut into fine lasagne or 200g (7oz) dried lasagne

2 **green** or **red peppers**, deseeded and sliced

2 fresh **red** or **green chillies**, deseeded and cut into strips (optional)

500g (1lb 2oz) **courgettes**, cut into little finger-sized sticks

300g (10½oz) frozen **sweetcorn kernels**

150ml (¼ pint) plain **fromage frais**

2 tablespoons grated **parmesan cheese** (optional)

Pasta Parcels with Pumpkin, Prawns and Ginger with a Leek Sauce

The sweetness of the pumpkin marries well with the prawns in these little pasta parcels, which come with a creamy leek sauce. A stunning dish for the autumn.

Makes about 1kg (2¼lb) ravioli (about 40)

Serves 4
as a main dish or
Serves 8 *as a starter*

1 *quantity* **fresh pasta dough**
(see recipe on page 78)

plain flour, *for dusting*

2 **fish** *or* **chicken stock cubes**

FOR THE FILLING

25g (1oz) **butter**

1 **shallot**, *finely chopped*

600g (1lb 5oz) **pumpkin flesh** *(peeled and deseeded weight), roughly chopped*

salt and freshly ground black pepper

2-3 *teaspoons* **ground ginger**

20 *fresh raw* **prawns**, *shelled and halved*

(continued overleaf)

Make the pasta dough and allow it to rest while you are preparing the ingredients for filling the parcels.

For the filling, melt the butter in a heavy-based saucepan and sweat the shallot in the butter without allowing it to brown. Stir in the pumpkin flesh, salt and pepper and ginger. Cover and cook gently for about 20 minutes or until quite soft.

Uncover, increase the heat and mash the mixture with a potato masher to make a rough purée. Cook briskly until all excess moisture has evaporated, stirring occasionally. Remove the pan from the heat and set aside to cool.

Make the ravioli. Work with half the pasta at a time: cut the dough in half, cover one half and set it aside. Roll out the other half to a very thin sheet approximately 45x55cm (17½ x21½in) in size – about the size of a teatowel.

Place teaspoon-sized mounds of half the pumpkin mixture, well-spaced out, over half the surface of the pasta. Top each mound with half a prawn. Wet the spaces of pasta between the mounds. Bring the other half of the pasta up and over the pumpkin mixture and press it down well in between the mounds.

Cut out raviolis the size and shape required (square, round, and so on) with a pasta cutter, scone cutter or sharp knife. Press the edges together well to seal them. Repeat the process with the remaining dough and filling. Flour the finished ravioli well, put them quite well spaced out on a tray or rack lined with non-stick baking parchment and refrigerate (or freeze) until required.

FOR THE SAUCE

25g (1oz) **butter**

2 small **leeks**, washed
and thinly sliced

250ml (9fl oz) **water** or
fish or chicken stock

250ml (9fl oz)
crème fraîche

thinly sliced **spring
onions**, to garnish

For the sauce, melt the butter in a saucepan, add the leeks with some salt and pepper and cook gently until softened, without allowing them to brown. Put the mixture into a blender or food processor with the water or stock and blend to a smooth purée. Return to the pan and simmer for 2-3 minutes, then stir in the crème fraîche and simmer for a minute or two more. Check and adjust the seasoning.

Meanwhile, bring a huge pan of water to the boil – a preserving pan works well. Crumble in the stock cubes, stirring until dissolved. Drop in the ravioli and boil for 3-4 minutes or until just tender. Taste the edges of the pasta parcels to see if they are cooked. Drain well.

Either serve the ravioli on warmed plates with some leek sauce poured over, or put them into a large bowl and bathe in the sauce. Garnish with spring onions.

Ravioli of Choucroute with Fresh and Smoked Salmon

Fish with choucroute (sauerkraut) is not nearly as modern nor as original as many young Alsatian chefs would have us believe: sixteenth-century Alsace cookbooks give recipes for the combination, often recommended for days of fasting. A lovely dish for those who like to play with their food – it's quite laborious to make, but both ravioli and sauce can be prepared ahead, leaving you with just 5 minutes' poaching and a brief reheating of the sauce.

**Makes 16 large
(8cm/3¼in) ravioli,
serving 3-4**
as a main course

1 quantity
fresh pasta dough
(see recipe on page 78)

plain flour, for dusting

(continued on opposite page)

Make the pasta dough, wrap in foil and allow it to rest while you prepare the filling.

For the filling, squeeze out the sauerkraut to get rid of any excess moisture and put it in a bowl. Stir in the fresh salmon and the smoked salmon. Mix the egg yolk (reserve the white) with the cream and juniper berries and add it to the fish and sauerkraut. Stir to mix, then season to taste with black pepper only. Set the filling aside while you roll out the pasta dough.

Cut the pasta dough in half. Put one half back in the foil. Working on a large, lightly floured working surface, roll out the other half thinly to a rectangle about the size of a teatowel. Arrange 8 heaped tablespoons of half the fish filling, well-spaced out, over half the surface of the pasta.

Brush the spaces of dough between the filling with the reserved lightly beaten egg white, lift the unfilled side of pasta up and over to cover the heaps of filling. Press down in between the mounds to seal and to expel air. Cut out ravioli with an 8cm (3¼in) scone cutter or sharp knife.

Dust the ravioli generously with flour and put them on a large tray. Refrigerate while making the remaining ravioli. Repeat with the remaining pasta dough and filling to make 8 more ravioli (you can re-cycle any leftover dough into fine noodles – see recipe on page 78).

For the sauce, melt the butter in a pan and soften the shallot in the butter without allowing it to brown. Add the fish stock and cook briskly until reduced by half. Add the wine and cook briskly again until reduced by half. Whisk in the cream and cook briskly once more until reduced by half. Taste and adjust the seasoning. Everything can be prepared ahead up to this point and set aside for a few hours (but not more than 3-4 hours, or the pasta will become too soft).

Bring a large, wide pan of salted water to a simmer. Poach the ravioli gently in the water for 3-4 minutes or until just tender. Fish one out, cut a piece off the doubled edge (the part that takes longest to cook) and taste – if it is still a little hard, continue cooking until it is done. Drain well. Reheat the sauce until piping hot and spoon it over the cooked ravioli.

FOR THE FILLING

200g (7oz) cooked **sauerkraut** (canned, frozen or sous-vide)

200g (7oz) skinless, boneless fresh **salmon fillet**, diced

100g (3½oz) **smoked salmon**, finely diced

1 **egg**, separated

2-3 tablespoons **whipping cream**

6 dried **juniper berries**, flattened with the side of a knife blade

salt and freshly ground black pepper

FOR THE SAUCE

25g (1oz) **butter**

1 **shallot**, finely chopped

300ml (½ pint) **fish stock**

300ml (½ pint) **dry white wine**

150ml (¼ pint) **whipping cream**

Pasta with Rocket, Raw Mushrooms and Shaved parmesan

A quick and delicious pasta dish, lovely for supper in the kitchen. It's important that the pasta is of the finest and the button mushrooms are very thinly sliced, otherwise the dish can become a little clumsy.

Cook the pasta in a large pan of boiling, salted water until just tender – 3-4 minutes if fresh (follow the packet instructions if dried).

Drain well and return it to the pan with the olive oil, mushrooms and salt and pepper, tossing carefully to mix.

Divide among 4 warmed plates or soup bowls, sprinkle with rocket and arrange shaved curls of parmesan cheese on top. Serve.

Serves 3-4

1 quantity **fresh pasta dough** (see recipe on page 78) cut into fine noodles, or 300g (10½oz) dried tagliatelle or paglia e fieno

salt and freshly ground black pepper

2-3 tablespoons **olive oil**

100g (3½oz) **button mushrooms**, very thinly sliced

a good handful of **rocket leaves** (about 50g/1¾oz), chopped

50g (1¾oz) shaved **parmesan cheese**

*B*eans have always had a troublesome reputation. Pythagoras wouldn't touch them, while Saint Augustine thought that the wind they produced served as confirmation of mankind's less-than-perfect nature and that they should therefore be avoided. Saint Jerome, it seems, expressly forbade their consumption by the nuns in his care; he considered that the resulting flatulence might titillate certain parts of the conventual body, which would best be left undisturbed.

It seems that the human gut lacks the enzymes necessary to deal with the carbohydrates contained in beans. To counteract this, some cooks soak the beans for several hours and discard the soaking water before cooking as a way of getting round the problem. I must admit, I never bother – it's one more thing to remember, it seems to make little difference to the cooking time (or indeed to the wind factor) and I'm always afraid of losing flavour by throwing away the soaking water.

The use of certain herbs or spices is said to help the digestion of beans – Mexicans favour epazote (*Chenopodium ambrosioides* or wormseed), while the Swiss and Germans use winter savory (alias *Bohnenkraut*, the 'bean herb'). In India, asafoetida, turmeric or ginger would be used to the same effect.

B E A N S

chick peas & lentils

Pot Beans, Mexican-Style

'Pot beans' is the literal translation of frijoles de olla, the brilliant Mexican way of doing beans. Once cooked and cooled, the beans are refrigerated for at least a day to allow the flavours to ripen. Prepared in this way they will be richly flavoured, slightly soupy and quite irresistible.

In Mexico, black or pinto beans are the most commonly used, but the same system can be applied to all other kinds of dried beans. Try white haricot beans with olive oil, a fresh red chilli and a chopped tomato; or flageolets with butter, tarragon and sliced leek; or red kidney or pinto beans with chilli oil, ginger, turmeric and tomato; or butter beans with oil, lemon grass and coriander. Variations are endless.

Makes about 1.6kg (3½lb) pot beans, serving 8-10

FOR SIMMERING THE BEANS

500g (1lb 2oz) **dried beans** (see notes above)

1 **onion**, peeled and quartered

1 clove **garlic**, peeled and left whole

1 tablespoon **olive oil**

1 fresh or dried **chilli**, left whole (optional)

a sprig of fresh **herbs** such as epazote, winter savory, tarragon, sage or lovage or a piece of fresh root ginger or a pinch of cumin seeds

(continued on opposite page)

Put the beans in a large saucepan and add 2 litres (3½ pints) water. Add the onion, garlic, oil, chilli, if using, and the chosen herb or other flavouring. Bring rapidly to a rolling boil, then turn down the heat and simmer, covered, for about 1 hour – it is impossible to be precise on timing, as this depends on how long the beans have been lurking on your (or someone else's) shelf. You may need to add up to 500ml (18fl oz) more water during this time. Test the beans after 1 hour: lift out a spoonful, blow on them and they should wrinkle and the skins break open. If not, continue cooking.

For the final fry-up, when the beans are almost ready (as described above), heat the oil in a heavy-based frying pan and fry the onion, garlic and chilli, if using, in the oil until lightly golden. Stir in the tomato flesh, if using, and cook briskly to reduce the mixture to a paste, stirring occasionally.

Increase the heat to maximum and equip yourself with a splatter shield or lid. Tip 2 ladles of beans with their juice into the pan and cover with the splatter shield or lid until the worst is over. Uncover and mash the beans into the pan with a potato masher or the back of a wooden spoon. Let them cook down to a thick paste. Season with salt.

Return this bean paste to the simmering pan of beans, stir in well, check the seasoning and add more salt if necessary. Cook for a further 20-30 minutes, stirring occasionally, then serve.

FOR THE FINAL FRY-UP

1 tablespoon **olive oil**

1 **onion**, finely chopped

1 clove **garlic**, crushed

1 fresh **green**
or **red chilli**,
deseeded and finely
chopped (optional)

2 **tomatoes**, skinned and
roughly chopped (optional)

salt

Bean Purées

If you purée your pot beans and fry the purée in a little oil you get what the Mexicans call frijoles refritos. You can use not only black or brown beans but also white, red or flageolet. The darker varieties go well with grilled or roast meats, particularly lamb or game. Purées from the paler, more delicate beans (flageolets, haricot, butter) make an excellent backdrop for white meats or fish. The chopped radishes (optional) give a good crunchy contrast.

Put the beans with their juices in a blender or food processor and blend until smooth. Heat the oil in a heavy-based frying pan (preferably non-stick) and fry the onion and garlic in the oil, allowing them to take a little colour.

Tip in the bean purée and cook briskly, stirring, for about 15 minutes or until the mixture is thick and pasty – so much so that you can roll it out onto a serving plate. Scatter the radishes on top, if using, and serve.

Serves 4

½ quantity **pot beans**
with their juices
(see recipe on opposite page)
– about 800g (1¾lb)
or 800g (1¾lb) canned
beans with their juices
(any colour)

1 tablespoon **olive oil**

1 **onion**, finely chopped

1 clove **garlic**, crushed

a bunch of **radishes**,
chopped (optional)

Bean Feast Tricolore

Canned beans are best for this lovely salad – home-cooked beans are too soupy. Try to find a good selection of beans – white haricots, red kidney and pinto or flageolets for instance – so as to get a good colour contrast.

For the dressing, put the garlic, sugar, mustard, onion, lemon or lime juice, oil, salt and pepper, mayonnaise and 2 tablespoons water in a blender or food processor and blend until smooth and thick. Set aside.

For the bean salad, rinse and drain the beans, keeping each type separate, and shake them dry. Arrange them decoratively in a deep bowl.

Pour the dressing over the beans and garnish with the avocado cubes, red onions and radishes. Alternatively, toss the mixed beans and dressing together and garnish as before.

Serves 8-10

FOR THE DRESSING

1 clove **garlic**, crushed

1 teaspoon **caster sugar**

2 teaspoons French-type **mustard**

1 slice of **onion**

3 tablespoons **lemon** or **lime juice**

150ml (¼ pint) **olive oil**

salt and freshly ground black pepper

1 tablespoon **mayonnaise**

FOR THE BEAN SALAD

two 400g (14oz) cans **flageolet beans**

two 400g (14oz) cans **kidney beans**

two 400g (14oz) cans **pinto** or **borlotti beans**

2 **avocados**, peeled, stoned and cut into small cubes

2 **red onions**, finely chopped

a bunch of **radishes**, finely chopped

Ragout of Flageolets with Leeks, Cream and Herbs

The slippery crunchiness of the leeks contrasts nicely with the yielding beans in this delicious dish, which is quite good enough to stand on its own as a supper dish. Alternatively, you can serve it with meat – it's especially good with barbecued lamb. Vary the herbs according to what you have to hand: chervil and tarragon are delicate, while basil, lovage and rosemary are more robust herbs.

Serves 2 as a main course or **Serves 4** as an accompaniment

500g (1lb 2oz) **leeks**

25g (1oz) **butter**

1 clove **garlic**, crushed

½ quantity **flageolet beans** cooked as in pot beans (see recipe on page 92) with their juices or two 400g (14oz) cans flageolet beans

200ml (7fl oz) **meat** or **vegetable stock**

plenty of finely chopped fresh **herbs** in season (see suggestions above)

3-4 tablespoons **whipping cream**

salt and freshly ground black pepper

Trim the leeks (leaving a bit of greenery) and cut into 1cm/½in slices. Wash them well to remove any sand, grit or dirt.

Melt the butter in a large heavy-based pan and cook the garlic and prepared leeks over a low heat, covered, for about 10 minutes or until just soft but not brown.

Drain the canned flageolets and add to the pan with the stock (or if using home-cooked beans with their juices, stock will not be necessary). Cover and cook for 10 minutes.

Remove the lid, increase the heat and cook briskly to evaporate the juices almost completely, stirring occasionally. Stir in the chopped herbs and cream and season to taste with salt and pepper.

Salad of Chick Peas, Spring Onions, Rocket, Feta and Black Olives

Chick peas came to us from the Mediterranean basin, where they are still an important part of the staple diet (their Latin name is Cicer; it seems that Cicero was so nicknamed because he sported a chick pea-sized wart on his nose). Extremely nutritious, they contain plenty of good carbohydrates, as well as protein, phosphorus, calcium and iron. They were said to be the marching rations for the invading Arab armies as they moved into North Africa and Spain.

Chick peas cook more quickly if soaked for 48 hours in the fridge (they must be refrigerated as they ferment easily at room temperature). Boil them for 1-1½ hours with onion and garlic, adding salt at the end. Even when thoroughly cooked, they retain an appealing crunchiness. 500g (1lb 2oz) dried chick peas will give about 1.2kg (2lb 12oz) when soaked and cooked.

A colourful, crunchy, southern salad, great for summer. If you cook the chick peas yourself, season them and add the oil and lemon juice while they are still warm.

Serves 4

500g (1lb 2oz) cooked or canned and drained **chick peas**

salt and freshly ground black pepper

6 tablespoons **olive oil** or herb oil

(see recipes on page 168)

juice of 1 **lemon**

1-2 **spring onions**, finely chopped, green part included

a handful of **rocket leaves**, roughly chopped

100g (3½oz) stoned **black olives**

100g (3½oz) **feta cheese**, diced

Put the chick peas in a large, shallow dish and season lightly with salt and pepper – remember the feta and olives and go easy with the salt. Stir in the olive oil or herb oil and lemon juice, turning to coat well.

Add all the remaining ingredients, stir gently to mix, then cover and refrigerate for an hour or two before serving, to allow the flavours to blend.

Zesty Chick Pea Soup with Mixed Vegetables, Green (or Chipotle) Chillies and Lime

A nicely spicy soup, great winter food: the base is a rich tomato sauce, to which is added stock, chick peas, sundry vegetables and, if liked, a good squirt of harissa paste.

Serves 4

1 tablespoon **olive oil**

1 **onion**, finely chopped

1 clove **garlic**, crushed

2 fresh **green chillies**, such as serrano, jalapeño or peperoncini, deseeded and finely chopped

400g (14oz) can **tomatoes** with their juice

1 litre (1¾ pints) **vegetable stock**

300g (10½oz) cooked or canned and drained **chick peas**

300g (10½oz) **courgettes**, diced

200g (7oz) **French beans**, cut into short lengths

3-4 pieces of **lemon zest**

salt and freshly ground black pepper

1 tablespoon **harissa paste** (optional)

juice of 1 **lime**

soured cream or plain fromage frais, to serve

Heat the oil in a heavy-based saucepan and soften the onion, garlic and chillies in the oil without allowing them to brown. Add the tomatoes and cook down to a thick purée, stirring occasionally.

Add the stock and bring to the boil. Stir in the chick peas, courgettes, French beans and lemon zest, season to taste with salt and pepper, then cover and cook over a moderate heat for 20 minutes.

Before serving, stir in the harissa paste, if using, and the lime juice. Serve a bowl of soured cream or fromage frais on the side.

Lentil Soup with Chiles Chipotle

A *great soup for winter. If you can't find the wonderful smoked chiles chipotle (available from Mexican speciality shops) substitute any other dried or fresh chilli to give the soup a bit of bite.*

Lentils are enjoying something of a renaissance. They were not always so popular – the Abbot Buchinger, author in 1671 of Alsace's most famous cookery book, claimed that they were 'no use, only for the servants, or for soup, or cooked like peas, with onions'. This valuable legume (second only to soya beans in protein content) is the one whose cultivation goes back the farthest: probably back to around 7000BC.

There are many different kinds of lentils, including the red (so-called Egyptian) varieties, the greenish-brown types used in France and Germany, and the decidedly pukka Puy lentils. I love their rustic flavours, which go well with all kinds of meat (especially game), smoked and salt pork and – a recent and delightful development – smoked fish. Their inherent richness can be counteracted to good effect by sharp flavours and seasonings like sun-dried tomatoes, lemon or lime juice, horseradish or chillies. Nowadays, there is generally no need to soak lentils before cooking – but check the packet.

Serves 4

1 tablespoon **olive oil**

1 large **onion**, *finely chopped*

1 large **carrot**, *finely chopped*

1 clove **garlic**, *crushed*

300g (10½oz) **Puy lentils**

1-2 dried **chiles chipotle**

salt

soured cream, *to serve*

chopped fresh **coriander**, *to garnish*

Heat the oil in a saucepan and soften the onion, carrot and garlic in the oil for 5 minutes. Add the lentils, stir until well coated with oil, then add 1.5 litres (2¾ pints) water and the chiles. Cover and simmer for 25-30 minutes or until the lentils are tender, stirring occasionally. Add salt to taste and simmer for a few minutes more.

Fish out the chiles, remove and discard the stalks, scrape out the seeds and chop the flesh finely. Put them in a blender or food processor with the lentil mixture and blend until smooth. Return the mixture to the rinsed-out saucepan and reheat gently until thoroughly hot.

Ladle into soup bowls to serve. Float some soured cream on the top of each serving and garnish with a little chopped coriander.

Warm Salad of Puy Lentils, Smoked Fish and Horseradish

Lentils have traditionally partnered all things smoked, particularly pork. Smoked fish is even more fun. Nowadays, lentils don't need soaking, so this makes a very quick dish to put together. If you think about cooking the lentils the day before (in which case they will be even tastier) and can find time to whisk up the dressing, the final reheating and assembly will take you about 5 minutes.

Rinse the lentils and put them in a pan with the lemon zest and juice, the shallot, peppercorns, bay leaf and 500ml (18fl oz) water. Do not add salt yet. Bring to the boil, then reduce the heat and simmer the lentils for 25-30 minutes or until just tender and the water is almost entirely absorbed. Add salt to taste. Remove the pan from the heat and allow the lentils to cool if not to be served at once.

Put the oil, vinegar, horseradish sauce, cream and salt and pepper in a small bowl or screw-top jar and whisk or shake vigorously together to make the dressing. Taste and see if you would like more horseradish and add accordingly.

Shortly before serving, reheat the lentils thoroughly and check and adjust the seasoning. Remove the pan from the heat and stir in the dressing. Divide the lentils among 4 plates or bowls and scatter some smoked salmon strips on top of each portion. Garnish with soured cream and chives.

Serves 4

200g (7oz) **green lentils** (Puy lentils if you can get them)

grated zest and juice of ½ **lemon**

1 **shallot**, finely chopped

1 teaspoon **black peppercorns**

1 **bay leaf**

salt and freshly ground black pepper

6 tablespoons **olive oil**

2 tablespoons **white wine vinegar**

1-2 tablespoons **creamed horseradish sauce**, or more if you wish

3 tablespoons **whipping cream**

250g (9oz) **smoked salmon**, cut into strips

soured cream and **fresh chives**, to garnish

I was lucky enough to grow up in north Yorkshire where fresh fish was plentiful and fishmongers two a penny. We holidayed on the north Northumbrian coast at Bamburgh, or in Scotland; occasionally we ventured south to Cornwall. We feasted on mackerel, mussels from the rocks, fresh crab from Seahouses, kippers from Craster and all kinds of fresh white fish, some familiar, others less well known. As my family were (and are) fishermen and -women, trout and salmon were frequently – sometimes too frequently – on the menu.

At weekends in our early-married, London-based days, we would wait on the bridge at high tide, after a round of golf at Rye, to catch the fishing boats coming back in with fresh codling and haddock. Later, I went to live in Spain, France and Mexico, and revelled in the wonderful fish markets there.

Nowadays, fish is all the rage – so much so that many of our oceans are being dangerously depleted and the price of most species has soared. The days are numbered, if not long gone, when fish could not be served as a main course when men were present as they would be hankering after 'good red meat' (to quote Jane Grigson in her *Fish Book*).

The following recipes feature many different kinds of fish and shellfish, some starters, some main courses, usually offering options for the kind of fish to use. Take a look at what is available, ask questions (if you are lucky enough to have someone to ask) and be a little adventurous.

The expensive, well-known varieties like sea bass, bream, sole, monkfish and turbot are easy to find and recognise, but don't forget the less grand grey mullet, coley, pollack and ling. Neither should cod be despised, though it must be sparkling fresh – and haddock is even better.

Once upon a time, salmon was a rare and expensive treat. Now, thanks to fish farming, it has become an extremely cheap food. (We are almost – but not quite – back to the days of eighteenth-century Basle when the salmon was so plentiful in the Rhine that servants would stipulate in their contract that they should not be forced to eat it more than once a week.) I love it, and find it immensely versatile, hence the rather large number of recipes for this and for sea trout. Some people complain that salmon is dry; it isn't – unless you overcook it. As many a Japanese gourmet will attest, fresh, healthy fish can safely be eaten raw. While you may not want your fish raw (except, for example, in the excellent Ceviches of Marinated Salmon on page 20), there's certainly no reason to cook it to the point of being dry and inedible.

F I S H
& shellfish

Juniper Röstis with Smoked Salmon and Horseradish Soured Cream

A pretty stunning starter or supper dish: individual crusty hot Röstis topped with cool slices of smoked salmon and soured cream lightly spiked with horseradish. The potatoes can be prepared ahead and the salmon sliced and ready for the last-minute frying and assembly.

Serves 4 *as a starter* or **Serves 2** *as a main course*

500g (1lb 2oz) *firm, waxy* **potatoes**

10 *dried* **juniper berries** (*or a handful of fresh dill, finely chopped*)

salt and freshly ground black pepper

olive oil, *for frying*

1 tablespoon **creamed horseradish**

4 tablespoons **soured cream**

150g (5½oz) **smoked salmon**

1 tablespoon finely chopped **red onions**

Start one day ahead: cook the potatoes in their skins in a pan of boiling water for about 15 minutes – they should remain quite firm. Drain, cool and refrigerate them overnight.

Peel and coarsely grate the potatoes. Crush the juniper berries using a pestle and mortar or under the blade of a knife. Mix them into the grated potatoes, or mix in the chopped dill, if using, with salt and pepper to taste.

Heat 1 tablespoon oil in a large, non-stick frying pan. Divide the potato mixture into 8 equal portions. Spoon 4 portions into the pan, pressing down each one with a spatula and neatening the edges, to make 4 individual Röstis, each about the size of a crumpet.

Cook until the underside is nicely golden, then turn the Röstis over and fry the second side. Remove from the pan, drain on absorbent kitchen paper, then place on a plate and keep warm. Heat a little more oil in the pan and fry the remaining 4 Röstis in the same way.

Stir the horseradish into the soured cream. Top each Rösti with some smoked salmon (fold it over if necessary) and finish with a blob of flavoured soured cream and some chopped red onions.

Fish in a Herby Crumb Crust

For this fine recipe, fish fillets are covered with a mixture of fresh herbs and breadcrumbs and briefly baked. A lovely dish for supper and quickly prepared.

Preheat the oven to 220°C/425°F/Gas Mark 7. Arrange the fish fillets in a single layer in a lightly oiled ovenproof dish. Season them with salt and pepper and set aside.

If you have a food processor, put the bread chunks into it and process with the herbs and a little salt until nicely crumbly. Through the funnel of the processor, add the oil, garlic and lemon juice and process until well mixed.

Alternatively, in a bowl, stir together the breadcrumbs, herbs (finely chopped), oil, garlic and lemon juice. Spread this mixture over the fish, pressing down well. Chill the fish until required, if liked.

Bake the fish in the oven for 8-10 minutes or until the fish is just opaque and the crumb crust is lightly golden. For an extra crusty finish, put briefly under a hot grill.

Serve with new potatoes, cooked fresh pasta tossed in olive or herb oil (see recipes on page 168) or broccoli florets.

Serves 4

500g (1lb 2oz) **white fish fillets**, such as haddock, cod, sole or turbot

salt and freshly ground black pepper

2 good slices of **bread** from a hearty loaf, crusts removed, cut into chunks, or 100g (3½oz) fresh white breadcrumbs

a handful of fresh **mixed herbs** such as basil, lovage, chives and marjoram, roughly chopped

2 tablespoons **olive oil**

1 clove **garlic**, crushed

juice of ½ **lemon**

Fish Fillets with Potato 'Scales'

Fillets of firm fish (such as haddock, turbot, monkfish, sole, halibut) are topped with potato 'scales', anointed with olive (or flavoured) oil and fried, potato-side down, until the potatoes are golden brown and the fish is just cooked. Serve with salad or broccoli.

Serves 2

about 200g (7oz) firm **potatoes**

300g (10½oz) firm **white fish fillet**

salt and freshly ground black pepper

olive oil, for frying

Peel the potatoes and slice them thinly. Season the fish with salt and pepper. Arrange the potato slices on top of the fish and place the fish on a plate. Cover and refrigerate until ready to fry, but do not leave them longer than about 1 hour, or the potatoes will go black.

Heat a little oil in a heavy-based frying pan over a moderate heat. Lift the potato slices off the fish and invert them into the pan. Put the fish back on top to fit. Fry until the potatoes are golden brown and cooked through – this will take about 10 minutes over a moderate heat (adjust the heat if necessary).

When the potatoes are brown and crusty, lower the heat and cover the pan with a lid or foil. Cook until the fish is just opaque – keep checking to make sure you don't overcook the fish.

Turn the fish out, potato-side up, onto warmed plates and serve with salad or broccoli.

Fishcakes with a Sharp Salsa

*T*raditional fishcakes are a fiddle: first you cook the fish, then you peel, cook and mash some potatoes, then you mess about with flour, egg and breadcrumbs. I wanted a recipe with minimal cooking and minimum fuss: just raw fish, leftover new potatoes and an egg to bind. You can use whatever fish you have to hand – salmon is good, or any firm white fish. The salsa (red onions, parsley, chilli and tomatoes) provides a cool contrast. If you can't be bothered with a salsa, serve avocado and lemon wedges to garnish.

For the fishcakes, finely chop the shallot in a food processor. Add the fish, potatoes, salt and pepper and herbs. Process in short bursts until the mixture comes together a bit – it should retain some texture; do not over-process or you will toughen the fish. Add the egg and process again briefly to bind the mixture together.

With wet hands, take handfuls of the mixture and shape it into 8 fishcakes. Put onto a plate and set aside, or cover and chill if not to be fried immediately.

For the salsa, finely chop the onions, parsley and chilli in a food processor. Add the tomatoes and process briefly until roughly chopped. Season to taste with salt and lemon juice, then put into a bowl and set aside.

Heat a little oil in a non-stick frying pan over a moderate heat and fry the fishcakes for 2-3 minutes on each side until golden and just cooked. Serve with the salsa.

Serves 2-3
(makes 8 fishcakes)

FOR THE FISHCAKES

1 **shallot**, quartered

350g (12oz) skinless, boneless **fish fillet**, roughly chopped

250g (9oz) cooked **new potatoes**, diced

salt and black pepper

plenty of fresh **parsley** (or chervil, dill or coriander), chopped

1 **egg**

olive oil, for frying

FOR THE SALSA (optional)

2 small **red onions**

plenty of fresh **parsley**

1 large fresh **red chilli**, deseeded

2 medium **tomatoes**, quartered

juice of ½ **lemon**

Moroccan Monkfish on a Bed of Saffron Couscous

In this robust recipe, monkfish is anointed with a North African-inspired marinade and baked on top of saffron couscous. You may need more than one monkfish tail to make up the weight.

Serves 8

2kg (4½lb) skinless **monkfish tail(s)**

1 teaspoon **coriander seeds**

2cm (¾in) crumbled piece of **cinnamon stick**

a pinch of **ground allspice** or quatre-épices

salt and pepper

1 tablespoon **harissa paste**

4 tablespoons **olive oil**

juice of 1 **lemon**

2 envelopes **powdered saffron** or 2 good pinches of saffron threads

500g (1lb 2oz) medium-fine pre-cooked **couscous**

1 **red** and 1 **orange pepper**, deseeded and cut into strips

500g **cherry tomatoes**

250g **asparagus**

400g (14oz) can **chick peas**, drained

fresh **coriander** or chervil leaves, to garnish

Put the fish into a large, shallow ovenproof dish. Set aside.

Put the coriander seeds and cinnamon in a small pan and dry-roast over a moderate heat for a few minutes, until they release their aromas. Do not let them burn. Remove the pan from the heat and grind the roast spices with the allspice and a pinch of salt, using a pestle and mortar. Stir in the harissa paste, 1 tablespoon oil and the lemon juice. Spread this mixture over the fish, cover and leave to marinate in the refrigerator for at least 1 hour and for up to 12 hours.

Preheat the oven to 200°C/400°F/Gas Mark 6. Put 500ml (18fl oz) water in a saucepan with 2 tablespoons of oil, 1 tablespoon salt and the saffron. Bring to the boil, then add the couscous in a steady stream, stirring. Remove the pan from the heat and set aside for 10 minutes, lifting and stirring the grains from time to time with a fork – the water will be entirely absorbed by the couscous.

Meanwhile, place the vegetables in a roasting tin and toss with a little olive oil and some salt and pepper. Roast for 30 minutes until softened and a little charred.

Turn the couscous into a lightly oiled ovenproof dish large enough to take the monkfish. Stir in the chick peas and check the seasoning, adding more salt if necessary. Put the fish on top of the couscous and bake in the oven for 20-25 minutes or until the fish is just opaque and the couscous hot.

Lift the fish off the couscous and onto a board. Cut the two fillets away from the central bone, discarding the bones. Slice the fillets and arrange them on top of the hot couscous with the roasted vegetables. Garnish with herbs.

Seared Fish Salad with Couscous and Green Pepper Vinaigrette

A quick and easy supper dish of gorgeous contrasts, with a Mediterranean feel about it: a highly coloured selection of fish (try salmon, white fish and scallops with corals intact) set on a bed of couscous and served with a vinaigrette with diced green pepper. The use of herb-flavoured oil (basil oil is especially good) will improve matters still further.

Put the couscous in an ovenproof bowl. Mix together 150ml (¼ pint) boiling water, 1 tablespoon oil and 1 teaspoon salt and pour it over the couscous. Stir to mix, then cover and leave to soak for 10 minutes. Fluff up the couscous with a fork, then cover with foil and put it in a low oven to keep warm for about 10 minutes, while you prepare the seared fish salad.

To make the dressing, put 3 tablespoons oil, some salt and pepper, the vinegar, mustard and sugar in a small bowl or screw-top jar and whisk or shake together until thoroughly mixed. Stir the green pepper into the dressing and set aside.

Cut the fish and shellfish into bite-sized pieces and dust them lightly with seasoned flour, shaking off any excess flour. Heat the remaining oil in a non-stick frying pan and fry the fish and shellfish briskly for 2 minutes – 1 minute on each side.

Divide the couscous between 2 plates. Lift the fish pieces out of the pan with a slotted spoon and arrange them with their juices over the couscous. Spoon over the green pepper dressing. Serve at once with crusty bread.

Serves 2
as a light supper

100g (3½oz) medium-fine pre-cooked **couscous**

5 tablespoons **olive oil** or herb oil
(see recipes on page 168)

salt and freshly ground black pepper

1 tablespoon **wine vinegar** or herb vinegar
(see recipe on page 169)

1 teaspoon **Dijon mustard**

a pinch of **caster sugar**

½ **green pepper**, deseeded and finely diced

300g (10½oz) mixed **fish fillets** and **shellfish** such as monkfish, salmon and scallops (weight without skin, bones or shells)

seasoned **plain flour**, for dusting

Barbecued Salmon or Sea Trout with Guacamole

A whole salmon or sea trout lends itself brilliantly to barbecuing, particularly if you have a kettle barbecue (with a domed lid). The size of your barbecue will limit the size of the fish – ours won't take anything much bigger than 1.5kg (3lb 5oz), and not more than 45cm (17½in) from nose to tail. Calculate 200g (7oz) cleaned fish per person, which takes into account waste. Remember: the only mistake you can make with salmon or sea trout is to overcook it – a 1.2kg (2¾lb) fish should not take more than 30 minutes, while a 1.6kg (3½lb) specimen may take 35-40 minutes. Take it off the heat in good time and remove a slice from the thickest part. If the fish is still a little underdone, serve the slices from the tail end first and return the rest of the fish to the heat until cooked to your liking.

Serves 6-8

FOR THE BARBECUED FISH

1.2-1.6kg (2¾-3½lb) **salmon** *or* **sea trout**, *cleaned, head and tail left on*

salt and freshly ground black pepper

sprigs of fresh **dill** *or fennel*

oil such as **herb oil** *(see recipes on page 168), for brushing*

FOR THE GUACAMOLE

1 fresh **green chilli** *such as serrano, jalapeño or peperoncini, deseeded and finely chopped*

1 clove **garlic**, *peeled*

4-5 sprigs fresh **coriander**

(continued on opposite page)

Heat the barbecue. Season the fish inside and out with salt and pepper. Tuck the herb sprigs inside the fish and brush all over with oil. When the barbecue is good and hot, brush the bars of the grill with a little oil. Lay the salmon straight onto the bars – there should be a protesting sizzle. Close the barbecue lid.

After about 15 minutes turn the fish carefully, using spatulas or fish slices. Cover again and cook the second side. After another 15 minutes, open up the fish and take a look inside – the flesh should be just opaque. If not, give it a little longer.

Meanwhile, make the guacamole. Crush the chilli, garlic, coriander and 1 teaspoon salt to a pulp using a pestle and mortar or blender or food processor. Add the avocado and lime juice. Crush to a pulp or blend or process in short bursts – the guacamole should have some texture. Stir in the spring onions and tomato at the end, if using. Transfer the guacamole to a bowl and press cling wrap tightly over the surface if it is not to be served immediately.

Remove the fish from the barbecue when it is cooked, put it on a serving dish and cover loosely with foil. Leave it for about 20 minutes at room temperature before serving it.

To serve, cut the top half of the fish into 3-4 equal-sized fillets. Lift out and discard the central bone, then cut the remaining fish into equal-sized pieces. Serve with the guacamole and garnish with lime slices and herb sprigs.

2 **avocados**, peeled, stoned and chopped

juice of 1 **lime**

2 tablespoons finely chopped **spring onions** (optional)

1 medium **tomato**, finely diced (optional)

Salmon or Sea Trout, Potato and Pesto Parcels

Delicate and delicious, these salmon parcels wrapped in brik pastry leaves (for which filo can be substituted) make a wonderful summer supper dish. The parcels can be prepared up to a day ahead, ready to be baked. No sauce is needed, but if you wish you can serve a bowl of plain fromage frais into which some fresh basil has been snipped. Ratatouille makes a good accompaniment.

Serves 10

6 new **potatoes**

10 brik pastry leaves or 10 sheets **filo pastry**

1 small jar (100g/3½oz) **pesto**

10 skinless, boneless salmon pavés or boneless **salmon steaks**, each about 125g (4½oz) in weight

salt and freshly ground black pepper

olive oil, for brushing

Cook the potatoes in their skins in a pan of boiling water for 10-15 minutes, or until just tender, then drain, peel and slice them thinly. Lay slices of cooked potato on each brik leaf or filo sheet – the potatoes should form a base the same size as the salmon.

Spread the pesto on the potatoes, then put the salmon on top. Season lightly with salt and pepper and bring the sides of the brik leaf or filo sheet up and over to enclose the filling and make a parcel.

Place on a baking sheet, seam-sides down, and brush with oil. The potato slices will be just visible through the pastry. Cover and chill if not to be baked immediately.

About 30 minutes before serving, preheat the oven to 220°C/425°F/Gas Mark 7. Brush the parcels once more with oil and bake in the oven for 10-12 minutes or until they are golden brown and just firm and springy to the touch.

Flaky Fish, Shellfish, Spinach and Tomato Pie with Brik Leaves

This is a sort of Mexicanised version of the Moroccan dish bstilla, which features pigeon (or quail) in a rich sauce, layered with brik leaves – with grateful thanks to Anissa Helou and the Restaurant Mamounia for inspiration. In keeping with the Mexican theme, you can serve it with guacamole (see recipe on page 116) and some boiled new potatoes, if liked.

For the marinade, finely chop or pound all the ingredients together using a pestle and mortar. If you have time, spread it all over the trimmed fish pieces, put them in a non-metallic dish and leave them to marinate in the fridge for several hours. Shell the prawns and set aside.

Preheat the oven to 200°C/400°F/Gas Mark 6. Squeeze out any excess moisture from the thawed spinach and chop it roughly. Melt the butter in a pan and soften the shallot and 1 clove garlic in the butter. Add the spinach, cover and cook gently for 5-6 minutes or until just tender. Season carefully with salt and pepper, then remove the pan from the heat and set it aside.

Meanwhile, process or chop the tomatoes roughly in a food processor or by hand. In a large, wide pan, heat a little oil and soften the onion and remaining garlic in the oil without allowing them to brown.

Increase the heat to moderate, add the tomato flesh and bouquet garni and season to taste with salt and pepper. Cook steadily, stirring occasionally, until the mixture is rich, thick and somewhat reduced – this will take about 20 minutes. Remove and discard the bouquet garni.

Oil a round 30cm (12in) ovenproof dish or cake tin which is about 6cm (2½in) deep and lay 10 brik leaves or filo sheets in the bottom like a rosette, brushing each one with oil – they should overlap and hang out over the edge of the dish or tin.

Serves 10

FOR THE MARINADE

2 cloves **garlic**, crushed

a bunch of fresh **coriander** (about 20g/¾oz), chopped

juice of 1 **lemon**

1-2 fresh **green chillies** such as serrano, jalapeño or peperoncini, deseeded and finely chopped

1 teaspoon salt

about 1.2kg (2¾lb) **assorted fish fillets**, such as monkfish, halibut, salmon and red mullet

350g (12oz) **prawns** in their shells

1kg (2¼lb) **frozen leaf spinach**, thawed

25g (1oz) **butter**

1 **shallot**, finely chopped

2 cloves **garlic**, crushed

(continued overleaf)

salt and freshly ground black pepper

two 800g (1¾lb) cans or four 400g (14oz) cans **tomatoes** with their juice

olive oil, for cooking and brushing

1 **onion**, finely chopped

1 **bouquet garni**

20 brik pastry leaves or 20 sheets **filo pastry**

1 **egg**, beaten

Spread the spinach mixture in the bottom of the pastry case, top with the tomato sauce and arrange the marinated fish and prawns over the tomato sauce. Brush the overhanging edges of brik or filo with beaten egg. Lay the remaining brik leaves or filo sheets on top of the pie. Press the overlapped edges together to seal, and bring them in over the top of the pie to form a rolled border. Brush the top with more oil. The pie can be prepared ahead up to this point, cooled, then refrigerated for a few hours before baking, if desired.

Bake the pie in the oven for 25-30 minutes or until the fish is cooked and the spinach and tomato filling is piping hot throughout. Stick a skewer in the centre to check that it is thoroughly hot; if not, continue cooking until hot. Serve.

Crab and Coriander Rösti

In this delicious recipe, crab meat comes together with grated potato, fresh coriander and shallots in a sort of savoury pancake. Serve with a cucumber salad.

Serves 2-3

300g (10½oz) **crab meat**

200g (7oz) firm, waxy **potatoes**, peeled and grated

2 tablespoons chopped fresh **coriander**

1 **egg**, lightly beaten

1 **shallot**, finely chopped

salt and freshly ground black pepper

olive oil, for frying

lemon wedges, to serve

In a bowl, mix together the crab meat, potatoes, coriander, egg, shallot and salt and pepper to taste.

Heat a little oil in a heavy-based frying pan and tip the crab mixture in. Press the mixture down with a wooden spatula and fry over a moderate heat for 5-6 minutes.

Put a plate over the top of the pan and invert the Rösti onto it. Heat a little more oil in the pan, then slide the Rösti back into the pan and cook the second side for a further 5-6 minutes, until cooked. Serve with lemon wedges.

Curried Clafoutis of Mussels, Monkfish, Scallops, Salmon and Bacon

If you're familiar with 'Toad in the Hole', you will know what this recipe is about: mussels, monkfish fillet, scallops, salmon chunks and bacon pieces are baked in a lightly curried batter for a sort of Toad-sur-Mer. Serve with salad.

Oil a 30x20x5cm (12x8x2in) or similar size roasting pan and set aside. Preheat the oven to 220°C/425°F/Gas Mark 7. Make the batter. Put the milk, flour, oil, eggs, salt and pepper and curry powder in a bowl or jug with 125ml (4fl oz) water and blend or beat together until thoroughly mixed. Leave to rest while you prepare the bacon and fish.

Sweat the lardons or bacon without any extra fat in a heavy-based frying pan over a moderate heat, until lightly golden. Do not fry them for too long, or they will become hard. Lift them out of the pan with a slotted spoon, put on a plate and set aside.

Dust all the fish pieces and scallops in seasoned flour. Fry them briskly in the bacon fat until just stiffened – a minute or so on each side. Put them in a colander set over the bowl or jug of batter to catch any rendered juices.

Scrub the mussels thoroughly and pull out the beards. Discard any that are not tightly closed. Steam them in a large, heavy-based, covered saucepan, without adding extra liquid, for 4-5 minutes, or until the mussels open. Once they are open, remove them from the pan and shell them. Discard any mussels that do not open.

Put the oiled roasting pan in the oven to get thoroughly hot. Pour in the batter and add the bacon, fish pieces, scallops and mussels, pushing them down well into the batter. Bake in the oven for 25-30 minutes or until golden brown and nicely puffed up.

Serves 4

125ml (4fl oz) **milk**

100g (3½oz) **plain flour**, plus extra for dusting

2 tablespoons **olive oil**

4 **eggs**

salt and freshly ground black pepper

2 teaspoons **curry powder**

200g (7oz) **lardons** or **streaky bacon**, finely chopped

150g (5½oz) **monkfish fillet**, cut into 2cm (¾in) pieces

150g (5½oz) skinless, boneless **salmon fillet**, cut into 2cm (¾in) pieces

150g (5½oz) shelled fresh **scallops**, sliced in half horizontally

500g (1lb 2oz) fresh **mussels** in their shells

Langoustines with a Creamy Lime Sauce and Avocado Chunks

A stunning dish for a special supper à deux: langoustines are briskly fried, and served with a lightly spicy sauce. At the last minute, avocado cubes are stirred in. This amount of raw langoustines (alias scampi or Dublin Bay Prawns) complete with heads, claws and shells looks like a lot. It isn't. Once you've got past the non-edible parts you only get about 250g (9oz) flesh. If you can't find whole ones (or prefer not to bother with peeling and stock-making), use shelled langoustines plus about 300ml (½ pint) bought fish stock. Serve with basmati rice.

Serves 2-3

1kg (2¼lb) raw, unshelled **langoustines**, heads intact, or 250g (9oz) shelled langoustines

1 teaspoon **black peppercorns**

1 **onion**, halved

pared zest of ½ **lime** or ½ small lemon

juice of 1 **lime** or 1 small lemon

a sprig of fresh **thyme**

1 **bay leaf**

some sprigs of fresh **parsley**

200ml (7fl oz) **dry white wine**

seasoned **plain flour**, for dusting

1-2 tablespoons **olive oil** or Kaffir lime leaf oil

(see recipe on page 168)

(continued on opposite page)

Get the stock-making and the reduction out of the way well ahead of time; this leaves only the very quick frying of the langoustines and the making of the sauce shortly before serving.

Using rubber gloves (the langoustines are prickly and quite an irritant), twist off the heads and claws. Pinch the shells firmly together and pull out the flesh.

Put the heads, claws and shells in a wide stainless steel pan (the width will aid reduction later) with 1 litre (1¾ pints) water, the peppercorns, onion, pared lime or lemon zest, juice of half the lime or lemon, thyme, bay leaf, parsley and wine. Bring to the boil, cover and simmer gently for 30 minutes.

Strain, discard the contents of the sieve and return the stock to the pan. Increase the heat and boil fiercely to reduce the stock to about 300ml (½ pint).

Shortly before serving, toss the peeled langoustines in seasoned flour and shake off any excess. Fry them very briefly in hot oil in a frying pan for a couple of minutes or until just firm and opaque. Remove them from the pan, put them into a serving dish and keep warm.

In the same pan, adding a little more oil if necessary, soften the shallots and chilli in the oil without allowing them to

brown. Add the stock and simmer for about 10 minutes or until further reduced and well-flavoured.

Remove the pan from the heat, then whisk in the crème fraîche, remaining lime or lemon juice and chopped coriander or chives. Stir in the langoustines and avocado cubes and bubble up briefly, before serving. Garnish with shredded basil leaves.

2 **shallots**, finely chopped

1 fresh **green chilli**, deseeded and finely chopped

3-4 tablespoons **crème fraîche**

plenty of chopped fresh **coriander** or chopped fresh chives

1 **avocado**, peeled, stoned and cut into cubes

shredded fresh **basil** leaves, to garnish

André Simon in his *Encyclopaedia of Gastronomy*, published in 1952, described chicken as 'just a barnyard fowl, and it may be rightly called the best of all birds covered by the name of poultry'. By 1974, Waverley Root was writing: 'A good many things taste like chicken except, nowadays, chicken, which tastes like damp cardboard.' So what could have happened in the intervening twenty years? We need look no further than the institution of intensive poultry farming, a new practice which rapidly grew in response to the demand for plentiful, cheap protein.

Nowadays, in our pampered Western society, many of us get all the protein we need and cheapness may no longer be the main consideration in choosing food. Happily, it seems that intensive chicken farming may be past its sell-by date. Let us hope that the time has at last come to get back to the barnyard fowl, free-ranging and fed, not on fishmeal and soya, but on maize, scraps from the kitchen and worms from the ground (it's a bit harder to find free-range quail and duck, but you may be lucky). Chosen carefully and well treated in this way, it need never again seem like the poor relation it has increasingly become.

Here is a collection of recipes using chicken breasts or legs, quail or duck, with influences as various as Mexico, France and Thailand. They are designed to convert particularly those who think chicken is not worth eating any more – and certainly not fit to be served to guests. Remember that poultry should always be cooked until firm and springy, and no longer pink – which does not mean that it needs to be cooked until dry, stringy and lifeless. Follow the recipe timings, but above all, check for yourself.

CHICKEN
quail & duck

Chicken and Mushroom Burritos with a Creamy Chile Sauce

For this recipe (which can be prepared ahead and baked at the last minute) strips of lightly fried chicken breasts and mushrooms are wrapped in a flour tortilla, rolled up and baked. A simple sauce (cream liquidised with some canned chiles chipotles) is added at the last minute, so that the tortillas remain crisp.

Preheat the oven to 200°C/400°F/Gas Mark 6. Season the chicken strips with salt and pepper. Heat the butter and oil in a frying pan, add the chicken and fry gently until just stiffened but barely cooked – a couple of minutes on each side. Remove the chicken from the pan using a slotted spoon and put it on a plate. Set aside.

Add the mushrooms to the pan, season with salt and pepper and fry gently until the juices run. Increase the heat and cook briskly, until the juices have evaporated and the mushrooms are quite dry, stirring occasionally. Remove the pan from the heat and stir in 3 tablespoons of cream.

Warm the tortillas briefly on a griddle (or in a frying pan or in the microwave), just long enough to make them pliable. Divide the chicken and mushrooms among the tortillas, roll them up and lay them in an ovenproof baking dish. Cool and chill the dish if it is not to be baked immediately.

Bake the tortillas in the oven for about 20 minutes or until thoroughly hot and crispy. Meanwhile, blend the remaining cream with the chiles in a blender or food processor, until smooth. Pour the sauce over the tortillas and return them to the oven for 5-6 minutes, or just long enough to heat the sauce a little without making the tortillas soggy.

Serves 4

500g (1lb 2oz) skinless, boneless **chicken breasts**, cut into finger-sized strips

salt and freshly ground black pepper

50g (1¾oz) **butter**

1 tablespoon **olive oil**

300g (10½oz) **mushrooms**, sliced

300ml (½ pint) **whipping cream**

eight-ten 16cm (6¼in) diameter **flour tortillas** (see recipe on page 161)

2 canned **chiles chipotle en adobo**

Chicken with a Red Pepper Sauce and Refried Beans

A whole chicken is crisply roasted, set on a bed of puréed beans (black, pinto or red kidney beans) and bathed in a creamy red pepper sauce. The contrast of the crusty golden chicken with the smooth, pale red sauce and the rustic bean purée makes this a very special dish; the colours are good, too.

Serves 4

1.3kg (3lb) **free-range chicken**

salt and freshly ground black pepper

a little **olive oil** or herb oil *(see recipes on page 168)*

100ml (3½fl oz) **chicken stock**

2 **red peppers**, grilled or roasted, skinned, deseeded and roughly chopped *(see page 13)*

1-2 fresh **red chilli(es)**, deseeded and chopped

250ml (9fl oz) **whipping cream**

juice of ½ **lemon**

bean purée *(see recipe on page 93)*, **to serve**

Preheat the oven to 200°C/400°F/Gas Mark 6. Season the chicken inside and out with salt and pepper and rub it all over with oil. Put it in a roasting pan and pour in the stock. Roast in the oven for about 45 minutes or until just cooked but still succulent, basting with the juices from time to time.

Meanwhile, make the sauce. Put the peppers in a blender or food processor with the chilli(es) and cream and blend until smooth. Set aside.

When the chicken is cooked, lift it out of the pan, put it on a plate and keep warm. Add the pepper sauce to the cooking juices in the pan and bring to the boil, stirring with a wire whisk. Season to taste with salt and pepper, then add a little lemon juice to sharpen the flavour.

Heat the bean purée in a frying pan for 4-5 minutes or until thoroughly hot, then put it into a shallow serving dish. Cut the chicken into 8 pieces and arrange them on top of the bean purée. Spoon some of the pepper sauce over the chicken and serve the rest separately.

Chicken, Red Rajas and Coriander Parcels with a Creamy Pepper and Tomato Sauce

Anyone who knows enchiladas will recognise the origins of this 'new Mexican' dish. Rajas (strips of roasted and peeled chillies and peppers) are enriched with cream, combined with shredded cooked chicken and coriander, parcelled up in brik pastry leaves or filo pastry sheets, brushed with oil and baked until golden. Use the chicken stock to make the rice to accompany this excellent dish and serve some black beans, too, if you like.

Serves 6

4 large skinless **chicken legs**, each about 250g (9oz) in weight

3 **onions**

1 **bouquet garni**

salt and freshly ground black pepper

2 **red peppers**

2-4 fresh **red chillies** such as fresno or peperoncini

3 tablespoons **olive oil**

200ml (7fl oz) **whipping cream**

3 tablespoons chopped fresh **coriander**

6 brik leaves or 6 sheets **filo pastry**

400g (14oz) can **tomatoes** with their juice

fresh **coriander** sprigs, to garnish

Put the chicken legs with one of the onions (peeled and quartered), the bouquet garni and salt and pepper in a saucepan and add enough water to just cover. Cover, bring to the boil and simmer gently for about 20 minutes.

Lift the chicken out of the pan, then remove the chicken meat from the bones, reserve the meat and put the bones back into the pan.

Shred the chicken meat and set aside. Simmer the stock for a further 30 minutes to extract maximum flavour, then strain and use the stock to make the rice. Discard the contents of the sieve.

Sear the peppers and chillies all over until thoroughly blackened and blistered, using a grill, gas flame or griddle. Rub off the skins under running water, remove and discard the cores and seeds and cut the flesh into thin strips. Set half of these pepper and chilli strips aside for the sauce.

Line a baking sheet with non-stick baking parchment and set aside. Preheat the oven to 220°C/425°F/Gas Mark 7. Slice a second onion and soften it with the remaining pepper and chilli strips in 1 tablespoon oil in a frying pan, until soft and the onion is lightly golden. Remove the pan from the heat, then stir in 2 tablespoons cream, the chopped coriander and shredded chicken.

Place some chicken filling on each brik leaf or filo sheet, dividing it equally among the pastry leaves or sheets. Fold each one over neatly into a parcel and place the parcels seam-sides down on the prepared baking sheet. Brush them with 1 tablespoon oil and bake in the oven for 10-12 minutes or until the tops are lightly golden and crispy.

Meanwhile, for the sauce, chop the remaining onion and put it in a blender or food processor with the remaining pepper and chilli strips, tomatoes and salt and pepper to taste and blend until smooth and well mixed.

Heat the remaining oil in a heavy-based frying pan and fry the sauce, stirring from time to time, until slightly thickened – this will take about 10 minutes. Whisk in the remaining cream, then check and adjust the seasoning.

Serve parcels over the sauce, garnished with coriander.

Lemon-Marinated Grilled Quail (or Poussin) Salad

A great recipe for a summer buffet: lemon-marinated quail or poussins are grilled, halved and served on salad leaves, sprinkled with edible flowers and set about with quail's eggs.

Wipe the quail or poussins with a damp cloth and remove and discard any extraneous heads, wing pinions, feathers, and so on. Put them into a large roasting pan which will accommodate them in a single layer. Mix together the lemon juice, oil, salt and pepper, onion and thyme. Sprinkle this over the birds, then cover and leave them to marinate for a few hours or overnight in the fridge.

If you have a combination oven, switch it to grill plus fan heat, and set the temperature at 240°C/475°F/Gas Mark 9; otherwise preheat the grill to high. Roast/grill the quail for about 15 minutes (poussins for 25-30 minutes) or until golden brown and just cooked. If you do not have a combination oven, roast the birds in the oven at 240°C/475°F/Gas Mark 9 and turn them once during cooking.

Remove from the oven, cut the quail in half and check that they (or the halved poussins) are cooked properly, and are no longer pink. If not, return the birds to the oven and cook for a few more minutes. Remove from the oven and leave them in the pan to cool off in their juices.

Put the quail's eggs in a pan of cold water. Bring to the boil and boil for 3 minutes. Drain, refresh in cold water, then peel and halve them.

For the dressing, whisk together the oil, vinegar, mustard, sugar and salt and pepper in a small bowl, then stir in any juices from the roasting pan. Arrange the dressed salad leaves on a large shallow dish, set the halved birds on top and spoon a little more dressing onto them. Arrange the quail's eggs in between the birds. Garnish with flowers.

Serves 8 (or more, if part of a buffet)

FOR THE MARINATED QUAIL
8 oven-ready **quail** or 4 poussins split in half

juice of 2 **lemons**

4 tablespoons **olive oil**

salt and freshly ground black pepper

1 **red onion**, finely chopped

3-4 sprigs of fresh **thyme**, plucked apart

12 **quail's eggs**

FOR THE DRESSING
6 tablespoons **olive oil**

2 tablespoons **white wine vinegar**

1 teaspoon French-type **mustard**

a pinch of **caster sugar**

selected **salad leaves** such as oak leaf, red oak leaf, lollo rosso and rocket, to serve

some **edible flowers**, such as heartsease, chives and pansies, to garnish

Warm Salad of Grilled Chicken with a Peck of Red Pepper Salsa

A warm salad of robust flavours and vivid colours. The chicken leg quarters are marinated in olive oil, coarse salt and herbs, grilled until crusty and golden and served over mixed salad leaves. The accompanying salsa, drizzled on top for serving, is spiked with red chilli, with extra flavouring from either coriander or basil. Substitute guacamole (recipe on page 116) if you like.

Serves 4

4 **chicken leg quarters**, each about 200g (7oz)

coarse salt and freshly ground black pepper

1 tablespoon **herb oil**
(see recipes on page 168)

1 **red pepper**

1 fresh **red chilli** such as fresno or peperoncini, about 7-8cm (2¾-3¼in) long

1 tablespoon chopped **spring onions**

100ml (3½fl oz) **olive oil**

several sprigs of fresh **coriander**, or fresh basil, snipped with scissors

a selection of **salad leaves** such as rocket, chicory, curly endive, lollo rosso and oakleaf, to serve

Trim the chicken leg quarters of any excess fat or skin (but do not skin them entirely). If you're in the mood, you can remove the bone from the thigh end, up to where it meets the leg joint. Season the chicken leg quarters with salt and pepper and sprinkle with herb oil. Put them in a shallow dish, then cover and leave to marinate in the fridge for several hours or overnight.

For the salsa, grill the pepper and the chilli as instructed on page 13. Rub off the skins and rinse under running water. Remove and discard the seeds from both. Put the flesh in a blender or food processor with the spring onions and salt to taste. Blend in short bursts until roughly chopped. Add the olive oil and blend until just mixed – the salsa should retain some texture. Check and adjust the seasoning, then tip the salsa into a small bowl; cover and refrigerate until required.

Preheat the grill to high. Put the chicken leg quarters on a rack in a grill pan and grill until golden and crusty – about 10-12 minutes on each side, depending on your heat source. Turn often to ensure even cooking. If they are getting too frazzled too early, set the legs further away from the heat source. They are ready when the juices run clear if pricked with a skewer at the thickest part. Let them rest for a few minutes before serving.

Stir the snipped herbs into the salsa. Arrange a bed of salad leaves on a large round platter and set the hot chicken in the middle. Spoon the salsa over the chicken pieces.

Chicken Breasts with Creamy Ginger, Lemon Grass and Coriander Sauce

A Thai-inspired chicken dish, just right for summer with its light fresh flavours. Serve with basmati rice or fresh pasta.

Season the chicken breasts lightly with salt and pepper. Heat the oil and butter in a frying pan or sauteuse large enough to take the chicken breasts in a single layer. Add the chicken and fry for a minute or so on each side – just enough to sear and colour them lightly. Lift them out of the pan, put them on a plate and set aside.

In the same pan, soften the garlic gently without allowing it to brown. Add the stock, ginger and lemon grass. Put the chicken pieces and any juices back into the pan, cover and simmer very gently for 10-12 minutes or until just firm and no longer pink – do not overcook or they will be dry.

Remove the breasts from the pan, put them on a plate, cover and keep them warm in a low oven. Strain the cooking liquid, discard the solids and return the liquid to the pan. Boil it down briskly to reduce to about one cupful.

Whisk in the crème fraîche using a wire whisk. Bring back to a brisk boil to reduce again to about one cupful of sauce. Check and adjust the seasoning. Return the chicken pieces to the pan for a final bubble up together with the sauce. Serve sprinkled with chopped coriander.

Serves 6

6 skinless, boneless **chicken breasts**

salt and freshly ground black pepper

1 tablespoon **olive oil**

25g (1oz) **butter**

1 clove **garlic**, crushed

300ml (½ pint) **chicken stock**

a walnut-sized piece of **fresh root ginger**, peeled and cut into pieces

4 stalks **lemon grass**, cut into 2cm (¾in) lengths

250ml (9fl oz) **crème fraîche**

a small bunch of fresh **coriander**, roughly chopped, to serve

Marinated Sweet-Sour Duck Breasts with Lime Butter Sauce

A delicious (but definitely last-minute) dish in which the sweet-sour lime butter sauce makes a good contrast to the rich duck. Serve with Herby Roast Vegetables (see recipe on page 38).

Trim the duck breasts of any gristle or fat but leave the skin on. Rub some salt and pepper into the duck well, especially into the skin, and put them into a shallow, non-metallic dish. Mix together the honey, soy sauce, ginger and the juice of 1 lime and pour it over the breasts. Cover and leave them to marinate in the refrigerator for at least 6 hours.

Preheat the grill to high. Lift the breasts out of the marinade. Reserve the marinade. Set the breasts on a rack over a roasting pan and put about 2cm (¾in) water in the pan (to prevent the fat burning). Grill the breasts for 5-6 minutes on each side, until just cooked. Remove from the grill, put them in a dish, then cover and keep warm in a low oven.

Peel the remaining 2 limes à vif (down to the flesh, leaving no white pith) and cut out the segments with a small sharp knife. Melt 25g (1oz) butter in a shallow pan. Fry the lime segments gently on both sides, turning once, then put them in the dish with the duck. Keep warm.

In the same pan, soften the shallots gently without allowing them to brown. Add the stock and reserved marinade. Boil hard to reduce the sauce to about 125ml (4fl oz). Cut the remaining butter into cubes. Remove the pan from the heat and beat in the butter cubes with a wire whisk until the sauce turns into a thick, creamy emulsion. Season to taste with salt and pepper.

Cut the duck into fairly thick, slanting slices and arrange on warmed serving plates. Garnish with lime segments. Drizzle a little sauce on top of the duck and serve the rest of the sauce separately.

Serves 6-8

4 **duck breasts** with skin on, each about 350g (12oz) in weight

salt and freshly ground black pepper

2 tablespoons runny **honey**

1 teaspoon **soy sauce**

a walnut-sized piece of **fresh root ginger**, peeled and grated

3 **limes**

100g (3½oz) **butter**, well-chilled

2 **shallots**, finely chopped

250ml (9fl oz) **chicken stock**

Stir-fried Duck with Ginger, Garlic, Broccoli, Carrots and Chinese Leaves

Make sure all the vegetables and meat are cut into thin strips of equal thickness and size so that they cook through quickly and evenly. Soured cream is an unorthodox but delicious accompaniment to this dish.

Serves 2-3

3 **carrots**, about 250g (9oz) in weight

200g (7oz) **broccoli**

300g (10½oz) **Chinese leaves**

1 **duck breast** with skin on, about 350g (12oz) in weight

1 tablespoon **olive oil**

1 clove **garlic**, crushed

a walnut-sized piece of **fresh root ginger**, peeled and thinly sliced

2 tablespoons **soy sauce**

salt and freshly ground black pepper

a bowl of **soured cream**, to serve (optional)

Peel and quarter the carrots lengthways, then cut the quarters into thin strips 4-5cm (1½-2in) long – somewhere between the size of a matchstick and a chip. Peel the broccoli stalks, divide into small florets, further dividing them if they are still significantly larger than the carrot pieces. Shred the Chinese leaves fairly thinly. Set aside.

With a sharp knife, cut the skin away from the duck breast as if skinning a fillet of fish. Cut the meat into strips and set aside. (The skin can be diced and fried in a pan over a moderate heat, until the fat is rendered and the skin thoroughly crispy. Lift out, drain on absorbent kitchen paper and scatter the crispy bits over a salad, or work them into bread dough. Use the fat for frying eggs or for another purpose. Fearfully bad for you, but rather wonderful.)

Heat the oil in a wok over a fairly fierce heat. Briefly stir-fry the garlic and ginger, then add the carrots and broccoli and stir-fry for 5-6 minutes, or until they are just beginning to droop a little. Taste them – they should be crunchy-tender but not raw. Add a little water if they start to brown but are not yet cooked to your liking.

Allow any water to evaporate before adding the Chinese leaves and keep everything moving around the pan. At the end, toss in the duck strips and cook only until they are opaque. Stir in the soy sauce and check the seasoning, adding salt and pepper, if necessary. Serve at once with a bowl of soured cream, if liked.

As recently as 1984, Harold McGee wrote (in *On Food and Cooking*) that 'meat has a special place in the diet of the Western world. For most of us, it is the main attraction of a meal'. Not any more – or anyway not for us, and perhaps not for you if you have bought this book. What a contrast with Charles Carter's *Compleat City and Country Cook*, (quoted by McGee) published in London in 1732, which featured about 50 pages of meat dishes, 25 of poultry, 40 of fish but only 25 of vegetables.

There are various reasons for this trend: in most European countries, BSE has taken its toll either directly or indirectly, while both dietary and digestive considerations play their part in the decision of people to eat less meat. And for some, the fact that it takes eight pounds of grain to give one pound of beef is philosophically and economically unacceptable.

When choosing meat, bear in mind that a stressed beast gives tough meat, so the more humane the method of slaughter used, the more tender the flesh will be. At least one positive outcome of the BSE crisis has been the concept of 'traceability' – it is much easier nowadays to check on the beast's exact provenance, perhaps even on its diet. If you have access to organically grown meat, you may prefer to buy this.

Here is a very personal selection of recipes for beef, veal, lamb, pork and game. I like my meat (except for pork) rather rare and recipe timings reflect this fact. If you prefer it well-done, increase the time accordingly.

MEAT
&game

'Eighty-Degree Roast'

Here is a great way to cook meat, thought to come either from the Agnes Amberg cooking school in Zurich or from Electrolux in Switzerland, and which is recommended by various Swiss friends.

A single muscle roast of top-quality, tender meat is seared in a pan and then finished in a preheated oven at a low setting – about the heat you would use to bake meringues – or the top left-hand oven of a 4-door Aga. Use an oven thermometer to check the temperature. It is an extremely practical method as the timing is much less delicate than for a regular roast (up to half an hour more in the oven will not make much difference to the cooked result); there is also less shrinkage, the flesh remains perfectly succulent and the flavour is wonderful.

The only slight drawback is that the meat is not piping hot, hence the importance of pre-heating both the oven and the roasting pan, as well as the plates on which you serve it. It is also medium rare. To my taste, the lower temperature means that the meat's natural flavours are even more pronounced, but if you like red hot, well-cooked meat, this method is not for you. Alternatively, you may prefer to reserve the method for serving the meat cold (i.e. chilled), as in the Porko Tonnato recipe (see recipe on page 146).

Serves 6-8

1kg (2¼lb) **fillet of beef**, or boned loin of veal, or a roast cut from the leg (noix), or boned saddle, loin or haunch of venison, or boned loin of pork, or a roast cut from the leg

salt and freshly ground black pepper

1 tablespoon **olive oil**

sprigs of fresh **thyme**, rosemary or sage (optional)

Remove the meat from the refrigerator and leave, covered, at room temperature for 1 hour before you cook it. Preheat the oven to 140°C/275°F/Gas Mark 1 for 20 minutes. Put the chosen roasting pan in the oven 5 minutes before cooking the meat, to get thoroughly hot.

Meanwhile, pat the meat dry and season it all over with salt and pepper. Heat the oil in a heavy-based frying pan or casserole dish large enough to accommodate the fillet. Sear the meat all over until thoroughly and evenly browned and lightly crusted – this will take about 10 minutes.

Transfer the meat to the hot roasting pan and add the herbs, if using. Reduce the oven temperature to 80°C/176°F (lowest setting on your gas oven) and bake the meat in the oven for 1½-2 hours. For medium rare beef, veal or venison, a meat thermometer should read 60°C. Pork should read 75°C. Serve with the juices from the pan.

Butterflied Lamb with Mint 'Pesto'

A leg or shoulder of lamb cooks better on the barbecue if you cut it open, remove the bone and open out the flesh, like the wings of a butterfly. Also, large cuts of meat do best in a kettle barbecue with a domed lid. If you don't have one, it's better to roast the meat in the oven in your usual way. The mint 'pesto' makes an agreeable variation on the mint sauce theme. Herby Roast Vegetables (see recipe on page 38) go well with this dish, as do black beans cooked the Mexican way (see recipe on page 92).

Light the barbecue and let it get hot or preheat the oven to 220°C/425°F/Gas Mark 7. Cut the bones out of the lamb and open the flesh out flat (or ask the butcher to do this for you). Trim rigorously and remove and discard any extraneous fat. Season with salt and pepper.

Peel both cloves of garlic and cut one into slivers. Make incisions all over the lamb using a sharp knife and insert the garlic slivers into the incisions.

Cook the lamb on a rack over a well-heated barbecue with the lid on, or on a rack in a roasting pan in the oven, for 40-45 minutes, turning occasionally, until the meat is nicely seared but still slightly pink inside.

Meanwhile, strip the leaves from the mint and put them in a food processor with the second clove of garlic, 1 teaspoon salt, the lemon juice, oil and pine nuts and process to a paste. Serve with the cooked lamb.

Serves 6

a small **leg** or **shoulder of lamb**, about 1.2kg (2¾lb) in weight

salt and freshly ground black pepper

2 cloves **garlic**

20 sprigs of fresh **mint**

juice of 1 **lemon**

6 tablespoons **olive oil**

2 tablespoons **pine nuts**

Spiced Barbecued Racks of Lamb with Garlic and Parsley Sauce

Be sure to get the butcher to chine (saw off the base of the bones from) the racks, otherwise you will have trouble carving them into neat cutlets. Toast the coriander seeds briefly in a dry frying pan to release some of their wonderful aromas. Serve the lamb with Mixed Vegetable Couscous (see recipe on page 41). If you don't want any last-minute sauce-making, you can skip the sauce and serve the carved cutlets on a bed of Ragout of Flageolets with Leeks, Cream and Herbs (see recipe on page 96).

Serves 8

about 2kg (4½lb) **racks of lamb** (weight before trimming) making 18-24 cutlets

1 teaspoon **coriander seeds**, crushed

salt and freshly ground black pepper

olive oil, for brushing

1 head of **garlic**

a good handful of fresh flat-leaf **parsley**, leaves only

100g (3½oz) **butter**

2-3 **shallots**, finely chopped

1 clove **garlic**, crushed

200ml (7fl oz) **whipping cream**

fresh **parsley** sprigs, to garnish

Light the barbecue and let it get very hot or preheat the oven to 220°C/425°F/Gas Mark 7. Thoroughly trim the lamb of any excess fat or skin and set aside.

Mix together the crushed coriander seeds and salt and pepper, and press firmly into the meat all over. Brush with oil and leave in a cool place until ready to cook. Wrap the garlic head (leaving it whole) in foil and put it on the barbecue.

Grill the lamb on a rack over the hot barbecue or in the oven for 10 minutes on each side (for medium rare), and longer if you like your lamb grey, rather than lightly pink.

Remove the meat from the barbecue or oven, place on a plate or board and leave it to rest in a warm place for at least 15 minutes, loosely covered with foil. Leave the garlic on the barbecue – it will take about 35 minutes to get really soft.

Make the sauce while the lamb is cooking: blanch the parsley leaves in a pan of boiling water for a couple of minutes, drain, then refresh in cold water to set the colour and pat dry.

Melt 25g (1oz) butter in a saucepan and soften the shallots and crushed garlic gently in the butter without allowing them to brown. Add the parsley and stew gently for 2 minutes. Scrape the mixture into a blender or food processor, add the cream and blend until smooth. Season to taste with salt and pepper.

Strain the sauce, discarding the contents of the sieve, then return the sauce to the pan and simmer gently for 5 minutes. Remove the pan from the heat and whisk in the remaining butter, bit by bit – the sauce will thicken slightly.

Serve 2-3 cooked lamb cutlets per person on a little pool of sauce and garnish with parsley sprigs. Serve the barbecued garlic, broken into cloves, for people to slip out of the casings and smear it over the lamb.

Porko Tonnato

I love the idea of vitello tonnato *but I find veal expensive and rather insipid. Here's a variation using a succulent tenderloin of pork, which is cooked using the 'Eighty-Degree Roast' method (see recipe on page 142). Fromage frais replaces the traditional mayonnaise in the sauce, which lightens things up considerably. It makes a wonderful summer dish and is delicious served with various salads.*

Serves 4–6

1 **tenderloin of pork**, about 300g (10½oz) in weight

salt and freshly ground black pepper

125ml (4fl oz) **olive oil**, plus 1 tablespoon

sprigs of fresh **rosemary**

150g (5½oz) canned **tuna fish** (drained weight)

100ml (3½fl oz) plain **fromage frais**

juice of 1 **lemon**

lemon wedges, to serve

Season the pork with salt and pepper, brown in 1 tablespoon hot olive oil and cook with rosemary sprigs for 1 hour, according to the detailed instructions for the 'Eighty-Degree Roast'. Cool, then chill the meat thoroughly in the refrigerator.

Slice the meat very thinly in slanting slices and set aside. Put the tuna fish, fromage frais and lemon juice in a blender or food processor and blend until well mixed. Add any juices from cooking the pork. Pour in 125ml (4fl oz) oil in a steady stream and continue blending until smooth. Season to taste with salt and pepper.

Spread some tuna sauce in the bottom of a shallow serving dish, lay slices of pork on top, overlapping them slightly. Repeat the layers, finishing with tuna sauce. Cover and chill thoroughly before serving. Serve with lemon wedges.

Venison Wrapped in Filo

Venison is a rare treat – at least for most of us. Here it is seasoned with juniper berries, and seared and wrapped in oiled filo sheets. Good partners include a Purée of Pinto or Red Kidney Beans (see recipe on page 93) or Rösti (see recipe on page 106) with added juniper berries, and Beetroot, Carrot and Parsnip Terrine (see recipe on page 48).

Mix together the juniper berries, salt and pepper and 1 tablespoon oil. Brush this mixture over the venison, place it in a dish, then cover and leave it to marinate in the refrigerator for several hours or overnight if you have time.

Line a baking sheet with non-stick baking parchment and set aside. Preheat the oven to 220°C/425°F/Gas Mark 7. Heat a little more oil in a heavy-based frying pan and sear the meat very briefly on both sides. Remove the pan from the heat, place the meat on a plate or board and allow it to cool.

Lay 2 filo sheets together on a board or work surface, overlapping them slightly, to give a rectangle big enough to envelop the meat. Brush with olive oil, follow with 2 more filo sheets, more oil and the final 2 filo sheets.

Place the meat in the middle of the filo sheets, bring the filo up and over to enclose the meat in a parcel. Invert the parcel onto the prepared baking sheet so that the seams are underneath. Brush the top of the pastry with more oil. Chill the filo parcel at this stage if it is not going to be cooked immediately.

Roast the meat parcel in the oven for 12 minutes (rare), or 14-15 minutes (medium). Remove from the oven and let it rest for 10 minutes before carving.

Serves 4

6 dried **juniper berries**, crushed under a knife blade

salt and freshly ground black pepper

olive oil, for cooking and brushing

600g (1lb 5oz) **boned saddle, loin or haunch of venison**

6 sheets **filo pastry**

Spiced Roast Pigeon (or Grouse) with Couscous, Currant and Chick Pea Stuffing

This excellent dish looks to North Africa for its inspiration, with its spicy combination of couscous, currants and chick peas. It is best to slit open the breast and cut away the breast cage before stuffing the birds. This makes them easier to carve, and the bones can be used to make a little jus. Otherwise, just spoon the stuffing into the cavity, and spoon it out again for serving. A salad of blood oranges and finely chopped red onions goes well with the dish.

Serves 6

3 oven-ready **pigeons** (or grouse) each about 400g (14oz) in weight

salt and freshly ground black pepper

about 200g (7oz) soaked or cooked **couscous** (see page 115)

4 tablespoons canned **chick peas,** rinsed and drained

2 tablespoons **currants**

1 teaspoon **ground cumin**

1 teaspoon **ground coriander**

1 **egg,** lightly beaten

a little **olive oil**

If you are game to semi-bone the birds, slit open the breast along each side of the breastbone. Keep moving the knife down close to the breast cage on each side until you reach the bottom. Sever the joints where the breast cage meets the wings. Cut out the breast cage using scissors or game shears. Season the inside of the birds with salt and pepper and set aside.

Preheat the oven to 220°C/425°F/Gas Mark 7. Mix together the couscous, chick peas, currants, half the cumin, half the coriander, the egg and salt and pepper to taste. If you have boned the birds, fill each one with 3-4 tablespoons of stuffing, mounding it up a little to simulate the breast shape – do not overfill as the stuffing swells on cooking. Close the breast meat over the top, stitch the skin together with dark thread and big stitches.

Alternatively, push 3-4 tablespoons of stuffing inside the birds – there will be more than you need, as there is less room if you have not removed the breast cages. Put the surplus stuffing in an ovenproof dish, cook in the oven alongside the stuffed birds and serve it separately.

Rub the birds all over with oil and sprinkle on the rest of the cumin and coriander. Put into a roasting pan. The birds can be prepared ahead to this point and refrigerated, if not to be cooked immediately.

Roast the birds in the oven for 5 minutes with the breasts uppermost. Turn them over, baste them and roast for a further 5 minutes, breast sides down. Turn them right side up, baste again and roast for a final 5 minutes – this should be long enough for the breasts to be pink and juicy, and the stuffing hot throughout: stick a skewer into the heart of the stuffing and hold it gingerly against your cheek – it should feel hot. If not, continue the cooking a little, but beware of overcooking them, which would be a tragedy.

Remove the birds from the oven and let them rest at room temperature for 15 minutes. Put your hand over the breast and pull firmly on the thread (if you have gone in for stitchery); it should unzip quite satisfactorily. Cut the birds in half with a very sharp knife or shears and serve one half to each person.

I was glad when I learnt that the word 'companion' is derived from the Latin 'com' (with) and 'panis' (bread). Sharing a loaf with a favoured friend is indeed a happy business and good bread is one of life's great pleasures. Most of the places we've lived in – Mexico, Switzerland, Alsace – have a serious bread culture. Nowadays, Britain increasingly offers good breads.

Even though I live in a country where bread is wonderful, I still make my own – though I admit I baulk at making baguettes. Bread dough is great for working off frustrations, and bread-making is one of the most creative branches of cookery that exists – with home-made pasta (see recipe on page 78) a close second.

The main ingredient – flour – can be white, wholewheat or rye, used in various proportions and combinations. If you're lucky enough to live near a flour mill, you can buy a range of flours there. Where white flour for bread-making is concerned, in Britain look for strong white bread flour. In France and Switzerland, you need the unbleached, soft-wheat, high-protein flour known as *Type 55*. Liquids can be water, milk, yoghurt or beer. Seeds or herbs add texture and interest, both within the dough or sprinkled on top of the loaf.

The recipes include a basic loaf of yeast bread, on which there's almost endless scope for variations. In addition to yeast-raised breads, there are also a couple of tasty recipes to accommodate stale bread, plus some baking powder breads (cornbread and scones) and flour tortillas, the Mexican flat breads.

BREAD *etc.*

A Basic Loaf

Here is a basic loaf made from a mixture of flours and a good handful of seeds. The recipe serves as a blueprint and the detailed instructions can be applied to all subsequent bread recipes. By interchanging the flours (all white, or half white and half brown) and the liquid (all water, or mixed water and milk), you can vary the theme.

Makes 1 large loaf *or a* 'party bread' *of 20 rolls*

500g (1lb 2oz) **strong white bread flour**

100g (3½oz) **strong wholewheat (wholemeal) bread flour**

100g (3½oz) **rye flour**

1 tablespoon salt

1 sachet easy-blend dried **yeast** or 15g (½oz) fresh yeast

a handful of **seeds** such as sesame, sunflower, poppy, pumpkin or linseeds, plus extra for sprinkling

125ml (4fl oz) natural **yoghurt**

about 400ml (14fl oz) **warm water**

MIXING, KNEADING AND FIRST RISE

If making bread by hand, mix together the flours, salt, yeast and seeds in a large bowl (if using fresh yeast, there is no need to dissolve it; just crumble it into the flour as if working butter into flour for pastry). Make a well in the centre of the dry ingredients. Mix in the yoghurt and water and work up to a rough dough. Scrape it out onto a work surface with a spatula or dough scraper and knead the dough by hand for at least 5 minutes. It should be firm, springy and no longer excessively sticky to the hands. Work in a little more flour as necessary to achieve this state of affairs. Alternatively, if the dough is too dry and firm, splash on a little more water to loosen it.

When the dough is the right consistency, return it to the bowl, encase the bowl in a large plastic bag and leave to rise at room temperature for about an hour or until the dough is doubled in bulk.

If using an electric mixer, fit the dough hook and mix together the flours, salt, yeast and seeds. With the motor running, add the yoghurt and water and work up to a dough. Knead thoroughly until firm and springy. The dough should start to clean itself off the hook and off the sides of the bowl. Work in a little more flour as necessary to achieve this state of affairs. Alternatively, if the dough is too dry and firm, splash in a little more water to loosen it. Remove the dough hook, encase the bowl in a large plastic bag and allow the dough to rise at room temperature for about an hour or until the dough is doubled in bulk.

If you want to give the dough a second rise in the bowl, knock it down, encase the bowl again in the plastic bag and allow it to rise once more until doubled in bulk.

SHAPING AND SECOND (OR THIRD) RISE

If baking the bread in a tin, lightly oil a large loaf tin about 26x13x8cm (10½x5x3¼in) in size. Turn the dough out of its bowl onto the work surface, knock it down, then press it out to a rough rectangle the same length as the tin, roll it up to form a bolster and press it firmly into the tin. Leave to rise to the top of the tin – this will take about 20 minutes at room temperature. Spray or sprinkle the loaf with water and sprinkle with a few extra seeds.

If free-forming the loaf, turn the dough out onto the work surface and pat it out to a rough circle. Bring the edges up into the centre and press them firmly down. Invert the dough and cup your hands around it to form a plump ball. Place a sheet of non-stick baking parchment on a wooden board (or flour the board lavishly), slash the loaf once or twice with a very sharp knife or razor. Leave to rise on the board for 25-30 minutes or until somewhat recovered. Spray or sprinkle the loaf with water and sprinkle with a few extra seeds.

BAKING

Place a roasting pan full of water in the bottom of the oven (to give a steamy atmosphere and a good crust). If baking the loaf free-form, place a heavy (preferably black) baking sheet in the middle of the oven and sprinkle it with flour. Preheat the oven to 220°C/425°F/Gas Mark 7.

When the oven is thoroughly hot, shunt the risen loaf off its board onto the hot baking sheet. If baking the loaf in a tin or as rolls, place the tin in the centre of the oven. Bake the bread in the oven for 30-35 minutes or until golden brown and crusty; rolls will take about 25 minutes. The bottom should sound deeply hollow when tapped with a knife.

A Grainy Bread

A wonderful bread, though quite dentally challenging on account of the wholewheat kernels, so be sure to cook them until soft. Flat beer gives an interesting flavour and a good rise, but you can use water if you prefer.

Makes 1 large loaf

100g (3½oz) **wholewheat kernels** or **bulgur wheat**

1 tablespoon **salad oil**

400g (14oz) **strong white bread flour**

200g (7oz) **strong wholewheat (wholemeal) bread flour**

2 teaspoons **salt**

20g (¾ oz) fresh **yeast** or 1 sachet easy-blend dried yeast

about 400ml (14fl oz) **flat (stale) beer**

Put the wholewheat kernels or bulgar wheat in a small pan with 500ml (18fl oz) water, bring to the boil and cook for about 15 minutes or until the water has evaporated and the kernels or bulgar wheat are soft. Remove the pan from the heat, stir in the oil, then set aside to cool.

Follow the general instructions for mixing, kneading and rising the dough in the recipe for a Basic Loaf (see recipe on page 152), using the beer as liquid, and the cooked wholewheat kernels or bulgar wheat instead of the seeds. Then shape and bake as instructed, depending on whether you want the loaf free-formed or tin-shaped.

Herby Flat Breads

Focaccias – flat breads with added flavourings, sprinkled with olive oil and coarse salt – are wonderful with summer barbecues or buffets. Here is a basic recipe flavoured with herbs, which can be finished with various toppings. They are quick to make and quick to stale – so eat up quickly, or use up in a Bread Salad (see recipe on page 156) or Savoury Bread Pudding (see recipe on page 159). Stale crumbs are also good for toppings, as in Fish in a Herby Crumb Crust (see recipe on page 109).

Follow the general instructions for mixing, kneading and rising the dough in the recipe for a Basic Loaf (see recipe on page 152), using the olive oil and warm water as liquid and substituting herbs or spices for the seeds.

Oil a rectangular 40x30cm (16x12in) or similar size baking sheet. Punch down the dough and press it out onto the baking sheet, going well into the corners. Brush the dough all over with oil and sprinkle with the chosen topping.

Poke a finger into the bread dough all over the surface, to make indentations. Allow the dough to rise a little on the baking sheet while you preheat the oven to 220°C/425°F/Gas Mark 7. Put a shallow dish of water in the bottom of the oven.

Bake the bread in the oven for 20-25 minutes or until golden brown and a little risen. Lift up one edge to make sure it is cooked on the bottom. Lift onto a large chopping board, cut into squares and serve at once.

Serves 6-8

FOR THE DOUGH

500g (1lb 2oz) **strong white bread flour**

2 teaspoons salt

20g (¾oz) fresh **yeast** or 1 sachet easy-blend dried yeast

2 tablespoons **olive oil**, plus extra for brushing

about 300ml (½ pint) **warm water**

1 tablespoon dried **herbes de provence** or 1 tablespoon spices such as fennel seeds or chilli flakes

FOR THE TOPPING

1 tablespoon coarse salt

or 1 tablespoon grated **parmesan cheese**
or a handful of **olives**
or 1 **red onion**, thinly sliced
or 2 tablespoons **sesame seeds**

Salad of Stale Bread with Tomatoes, Peppers and Olives

Bread salad is a Middle Eastern staple, and it crops up in our household during the summer months about once a week. Leftovers from any of the previous bread recipes would be good: it's essential to use a bread with character, otherwise the whole dish dissolves into a formless mush. Thereafter, tomatoes, lemon juice and olive oil play vital parts. Peppers, cucumber and olives are also included in this one.

Serves 4-6

150-200g (5½-7oz) stale
crusty **bread**, crusts
intact

juice of 2 **lemons**

½ **cucumber**, peeled,
deseeded and diced

1 **red pepper** and
1 **green pepper**, roasted,
skinned, deseeded
and diced
(see page 13)

1 **red onion**, finely
chopped

1 clove **garlic**, crushed

4-6 **tomatoes**, roughly
chopped

a handful of **black olives**

salt and freshly ground
black pepper

125ml (4fl oz) **olive oil**

a handful of chopped
fresh **mixed herbs** such
as mint, coriander,
parsley and basil

Cut the bread into bite-sized cubes. Put them in a large bowl and sprinkle with the lemon juice. Add all the remaining ingredients, tossing to mix well.

Cover and chill in the fridge for a few hours or overnight, to allow all the flavours to blend, before serving.

Courgette and Basil Bread with Parmesan

This fragrant, golden-green bread goes well with any summer food. The grated courgettes give it a wonderful moisture, rather in the same way as carrots to carrot cake, or bananas to banana bread. Substitute 1-2 tablespoons of pesto for the parmesan, olive oil and fresh basil if this suits you better.

Makes one 27cm (10¾in) loaf

500g (1lb 2oz) **strong white bread flour**

2 teaspoons salt

20g (¾oz) fresh **yeast**, crumbled, or 1 sachet easy-blend dried yeast

1 **courgette**, about 250g (9oz) in weight

3 tablespoons grated **parmesan cheese**

1 tablespoon **olive oil**

plenty of fresh **basil** leaves, snipped with scissors (or 1-2 tablespoons pesto – see note above)

about 250ml (9fl oz) **warm water**

Mix together the flour, salt and yeast in a large bowl. Grate the courgette coarsely using a cheese grater or Rösti grater. Mix it into the flour with the parmesan, oil and basil (or pesto). Add the water and work up to a dough, following the detailed instructions given for a Basic Loaf (see recipe on page 152).

Knead the dough thoroughly for at least 5 minutes, either by hand or with an electric mixer with the dough hook fitted. Add sprinkles of extra flour if the dough is too sticky. After 5 minutes it should start to clean itself off your hands, or off the sides of the bowl. Add more flour if necessary to achieve this. Encase the bowl in a plastic bag and leave the dough to rise at room temperature for about 1 hour, or until doubled in bulk.

Oil a 27x13x7cm (10¾x5x2¾in) or similar size loaf tin. Knock the dough down on a floured board and knead it a little again. Pat it out roughly to a rectangle the same length as the tin. Roll it up into a bolster shape and pack it firmly, seam-side down, into the tin. Leave it to rise to the top of the tin – this will take about 30 minutes at room temperature.

Meanwhile, preheat the oven to 220°C/425°F/Gas Mark 7. Bake the loaf in the oven for 35-40 minutes or until golden brown and the base sounds deeply hollow when tapped with a knife.

Savoury Bread Pudding

I love these 'stratified' savoury bread puddings (strata to the Italians, ramequin to the Swiss) in which stale bread is combined with something well-flavoured – probably some tasty left-over – bound with a creamy egg mixture and baked until golden. Use this recipe as a blue-print and create your own combinations, depending on what tasty morsels you can muster from the fridge or store cupboard.

Put the bread cubes in a large bowl and set aside. Whisk together the eggs, milk, cream, mustard and salt and pepper, and pour it over the bread. Mix well together and leave for about 30 minutes so that the bread absorbs the liquid.

Preheat the oven to 200°C/400°F/Gas Mark 6. Brush an ovenproof dish lightly with oil. Spoon a layer of soaked bread into the bottom of the dish, top with the chosen flavouring and finish with the rest of the soaked bread. Sprinkle the parmesan cheese over the top. The pudding can be prepared ahead up to this point, covered and refrigerated, if not baking it straight away.

Bake the pudding in the oven for about 30 minutes or until golden brown and puffy.

Serves 4

4 good handfuls (about 200g/7oz) of stale **bread** with crusts, cut into cubes

3 **eggs**

300ml (½ pint) **milk**

200ml (7fl oz) **whipping cream**

1 teaspoon **Dijon** or **coarse-grain mustard**

salt and freshly ground black pepper

about 300g (10½oz) something interesting, such as **artichoke hearts** and **ham**, goat's cheese and sun-dried tomatoes, cooked mushrooms and chopped fresh herbs, sundry vegetables, sweetcorn and bacon, etc., etc.

2 tablespoons grated **parmesan cheese**

Cornbread with Chillies, Coriander and Cheese

I'm very partial to the American-style cornbreads, based on yellow cornmeal and leavened with eggs and baking powder rather than yeast. Here is a version using polenta and cheddar cheese; I've also omitted honey or sugar, as I find the corn provides enough natural sweetness. Serve it on its own with a herby tomato sauce or use to accompany roast or grilled meats. Like all baking powder breads (scones, soda bread) it stales quickly. However, as it is extremely more-ish, it is unlikely to sit around long enough for this to happen.

Serves 4-6

100g (3½oz) **plain flour**

200g (7oz) **polenta** or **cornmeal**

1 teaspoon salt

2 teaspoons **baking powder**

300ml (½ pint) **milk** or buttermilk

300g (10½oz) canned (drained) or frozen **sweetcorn kernels**

4 tablespoons **olive oil**

3 **eggs**

plenty of chopped fresh **coriander**

2-3 fresh **red** or **green chillies** such as serrano, jalapeño or peperoncini, deseeded and chopped

50g (1¾oz) **cheddar cheese** or similar hard cheese, diced or grated

Preheat the oven to 220°C/425°F/Gas Mark 7. Mix together the plain flour, polenta or cornmeal, salt and baking powder in a large bowl and set aside. Put the milk or buttermilk, sweetcorn, oil, eggs, coriander, chillies and cheese in a blender or food processor and blend briefly to mix. Stir this mixture into the flours.

Oil a 25x20x5cm (10x8x2in) or similar size shallow, oven-proof dish, tip in the mixture and smooth the top. Bake in the oven for about 35 minutes or until golden brown and puffy, and a skewer inserted in the middle comes out clean.

Flour (Wheat) Tortillas

It takes a while to get into the rhythm of making tortillas (rather like crêpes), so while you are at it you may as well make lots. They freeze well.

In a mixing bowl or food processor, mix together the flour and salt. Add the oil and water and work up to a dough. Knead or process well until firm, springy and no longer sticky to the hands.

Lavishly flour a work surface. Roll the dough into a sausage and cut it into 12 equal slices. Roll out each slice as thinly as possible with a well-floured rolling pin, rotating so as to get an even circle.

Heat an ungreased, heavy-based frying pan or griddle over a moderate heat and cook a tortilla briefly on both sides. Turn it over as soon as you see bubbles appearing on the surface. The cooked side should barely colour (little brown spots) and the tortilla should remain supple. If large black spots develop soon after the tortillas go into the pan or griddle, reduce the heat. Wrap the cooked tortillas in a teatowel as they are ready, then fill them as instructed in the specific recipe.

If not using the cooked tortillas immediately, allow them to cool thoroughly, then wrap them in a teatowel and put in a plastic bag. They will keep for 3-4 days in the fridge. Wrap in foil or plastic bags in batches of 10 for freezing.

Makes about twenty-four 20cm (8in) diameter tortillas or thirty 16cm (6¼in) diameter tortillas

500g (1lb 2oz) **plain flour**

2 teaspoons salt

125ml (4fl oz) **olive oil**

about 250ml (9fl oz) **warm water**

'The singer's approach to jam making,' claimed Patience Gray in *Honey from a Weed*, 'is the essential one – enthusiasm.' Jam should definitely not be a tedious and major production, nor a sort of panic response to a glut of something rather dull. Rather it should be a joyful affair, in which some intensely flavoured fruit is picked at its peak and briefly boiled up to a marvellous crescendo, its warm summer aromas captured for quick consumption. The use of quick-setting jam sugar with added pectin shortens the cooking time and ensures that the fruit retains all its flavour. In the following recipes, the proportion of sugar to fruit is rather less than the conventional '1 for 1' (1kg fruit for 1kg sugar, and so on.), so it's best to eat these jams up fast, and to keep them in the fridge once opened.

Herb oils and vinegars are a wonderful addition to the kitchen, great for vinaigrettes and for roasting or grilling. They are simplicity itself: handfuls of fresh herbs, spices or garlic are immersed in oil or vinegar to cover and left to infuse for several weeks. They also make wonderful presents – collect nice bottles as you go along and give them good labels and hats.

PRESERVING

instincts

Apricot Jam with Lavender

Here is a wonderful preserve made from warm fresh apricots and fragrant lavender, an idea inspired by Jean Bardet, who has the two growing and ripening together in his famous potager.

Makes eight 450g (1lb) jars of jam

2kg (4½lb) **apricots**, stoned and quartered

1.5kg (3lb 5oz) quick-setting **jam sugar** with added pectin

juice of 1 **lemon**

8 fresh **lavender sprigs**, flowers stripped off the stalks

Put a saucer in the freezer for testing the jam later. Put the prepared apricots in a preserving pan with all the remaining ingredients, stir to mix well and leave for several hours or until the juices run.

Bring the mixture to the boil, stirring. Once the jam has reached a rolling boil, boil for 5 minutes, then start testing for setting: pour a little onto the frozen saucer, wait a bit and then run your finger through it. A distinct channel should form – and stay formed. If it does, remove the pan from the heat. If not, return the saucer to the freezer and continue cooking the jam for a minute or two longer, then test again.

When the jam has reached setting point, pot it into warm, sterilised jam jars, cover tightly and invert the jars when hot so that the fruit falls and air is excluded from the top of the jam. Once cold, store upright.

Peach Jam with Hyssop

Peaches, like cherries, need a bit of pectin in order for them to set. For this, the lemon juice helps, as well as the sugar with added pectin. Hyssop, the biblical herb, gives the jam an intriguing flavour with its slightly bitter mintiness. You can indeed substitute with mint, if this is more readily available – or omit the herb altogether.

Put a saucer in the freezer for testing the jam later. Slice the peaches roughly and put them in a preserving pan with all the remaining ingredients. Stir to mix well, then leave to macerate for an hour or two until the juices run.

Bring the mixture to the boil, stirring. Once the jam has reached a rolling boil, boil for 5 minutes, then start testing for setting: pour a little onto the frozen saucer, wait a bit and then run your finger through it. A distinct channel should form – and stay formed. If it does, remove the pan from the heat and remove and discard the hyssop. If not, return the saucer to the freezer and continue cooking the jam for a minute or two longer, then test again.

When the jam has reached setting point, pot it into warm, sterilised jam jars, cover tightly and invert the jars when hot so that the fruit falls and air is excluded from the top of the jam. Once cold, store upright.

Makes six 450g (1lb) jars of jam

2kg (4½lb) **peaches**, skinned and stoned

juice of 2 **lemons**

1.5kg (3lb 5oz) quick-setting **jam sugar** with added pectin

4 sprigs of fresh **hyssop**

Bettlach Black Cherry and Redcurrant Jam

Our house is surrounded by cherry orchards. Their owners always have far more fruit than they can possibly deal with and usually they leave the ladders up when they have picked their fill, inviting us to take care of the rest. The redcurrants give the jam the extra acidity (and pectin) that cherries lack.

Makes five or six 450g (1lb) jars of jam

1.5kg (3lb 5oz) **black cherries**

500g (1lb 2oz) **redcurrants**

1.5kg (3lb 5oz) quick-setting **jam sugar** with added pectin

a knob of **butter**

Put a saucer in the freezer for testing the jam later. Stone the cherries and remove the stalks from the redcurrants. Put the fruit in a preserving pan with the sugar and stir to mix well. Leave for a few hours or until the juice runs.

Bring the mixture to a rolling boil, add the butter, then boil briskly for 5 minutes, then start testing for setting: pour a little onto the frozen saucer, wait a bit and then run your finger through it. A distinct channel should form – and stay formed. If it does, remove the pan from the heat. If not, return the saucer to the freezer and continue boiling and testing the jam until it reaches setting point.

Pot the jam into warm, sterilised jam jars, cover tightly and invert the jars when hot so that the fruit goes to the bottom and air is excluded from the top of the jam. Once cold, store upright.

Confit of Onions

My wine buying tends to veer wildly between 90-Francs-a-bottle splurges on wonderful things to squirrel away in the cellar, and optimistic forays into nameless offerings costing around FF20. Quite a few of the latter end up in this gorgeous deep ruby-red onion jam. It is served warm and goes wonderfully well with white meats and poultry.

Put the onions in a heavy-based pan, stir in the oil, salt and pepper, sugar, vinegar and coriander seeds, cover and stew gently until soft – this will take about 15 minutes.

Remove the lid, increase the heat, add the wine and cook briskly until the wine has evaporated, stirring occasionally.

Add the stock, bay leaf and thyme and continue to cook, uncovered, stirring occasionally, until this liquid has also evaporated and the mixture has the consistency of a chutney – this will take about a further 30 minutes, depending on your pan and your heat source.

Remove and discard the bay leaf and thyme, and check and adjust the seasoning. If it s to be served immediately, put the onion mixture into a small bowl. Otherwise, remove the pan from the heat and spoon the hot mixture into a covered screw-top jar (or jars) and seal. Cool, then store in the fridge. Reheat gently before serving.

Serves 6

500g (1lb 2oz) **onions**, thinly sliced

1 tablespoon **olive oil** or **herb oil**
(see recipes on page 168)

salt and freshly ground black pepper

2 teaspoons **caster sugar**

4 tablespoons **red wine vinegar**

1 teaspoon **coriander seeds**, roughly crushed

200ml (7fl oz) **red wine**

500ml (18fl oz) **vegetable stock**

1 **bay leaf**

2-3 sprigs of fresh **thyme**

Herb Oils and Vinegars

There's nothing very complicated about making your own herb oils and vinegars; success is assured if you follow a few simple guidelines. Take a Kilner jar or other wide-necked glass jar with a well-fitting lid. Put in the fresh herb of your choice, filling the jar fairly loosely to within a couple of centimetres of the top. Be sure the herbs are quite dry, otherwise they may go mouldy. Pour in enough oil or white wine or cider vinegar. The herbs should be completely covered. (Olive oil should be avoided, a neutral-tasting salad oil being best for the purpose, to allow the delicate herb flavours to come through.)

It's important that the herbs are well sunk in the oil or vinegar: if any are above the surface, mould can result. Close tightly, label and date the jars and put them in a cool, dark place for 1-2 months.

When they are well-flavoured, tip the contents into a colander held over a bowl or jug, pressing down to extract all the flavour from the herbs. Discard the herbs. Strain the oil or vinegar through a clean piece of muslin, a J-cloth or a nappy liner. Decant into bottles and cork them tightly.

Thyme and Lemon Zest Oil

lots of fresh **thyme**

zest of 2 **lemons**, pared with a potato peeler

oil, to cover

Basil and Garlic Oil

lots of green or purple fresh **basil** leaves, stripped off the woody stalks

4 cloves **garlic**, peeled

oil, to cover

Lemon Grass, Chilli and Garlic Oil

3 stalks **lemon grass**, trimmed and sliced

1 fresh **red chilli**, pricked all over with a pin

1 clove **garlic**, peeled

oil, to cover

Kaffir Lime Leaves and Garlic Oil

a bunch of fresh **Kaffir lime leaves**, stripped off the woody stalks

2 cloves **garlic**, peeled

oil, to cover

Ginger and Garlic Oil

2 walnut-sized pieces of **fresh root ginger**, roughly bruised

2 cloves **garlic**, peeled

oil, to cover

Chilli and Lime Zest Oil

3 fresh **green chillies**, pricked all over with a pin

zest of 3 **limes**, pared with a potato peeler

oil, to cover

Herb and Flower Vinegar

a good handful of fresh **rose petals**

a good handful of fresh **tarragon**

a good handful of fresh **fennel** (herb)

several fresh **nasturtium flowers**

4 sprigs of fresh **thyme**

2 **bay leaves**

white wine or **cider vinegar**, to cover

Lemon, Lime and Orange Vinegar

pared zest and juice of 1 **lemon**

pared zest and juice of 1 **orange**

pared zest and juice of 1 **lime**

white wine or **cider vinegar**, to cover

Spice Vinegar

a walnut-sized piece of **fresh root ginger**

3 cloves **garlic**, peeled

1 tablespoon **black peppercorns**

3 **cloves**

white wine or **cider vinegar**, to cover

Fresh Goat's Cheeses in Oil

Not a particularly original recipe, but a perennial favourite. If you can resist them for at least a month, they will be the better for it. As you use up the cheeses, replace them with fresh ones.

Layer the cheeses with the garlic and herbs in a 1 litre (1¾ pints) Kilner jar or large jam jar with a tight-fitting lid. Fill up with the oil. The cheeses should be completely covered. Fasten the lid tightly and refrigerate for at least one month before using.

For 20 mini-goat's cheeses

20 small fresh **goat's cheeses** about 400g (14oz) total weight

10 cloves **garlic**, peeled

plenty of fresh **thyme** and **rosemary**

about 500ml (18fl oz) **oil**

*D*essert, sweet, pudding – whichever term you use, the story's the same. It's the sweet surprise, the grand finale that comes once the stage has been cleared – the word dessert comes from the French *desservir*, meaning to clear away. For people who indulge only rarely in dessert, it is not enough for a pudding simply to be sweet. It has to be worth its calories, which means it must look wonderful and taste memorable.

The following is a selection of sweets which are both beautiful to behold and gorgeous to eat. Your choice will be influenced by the rest of the menu. If you have planned a light and uncomplicated meal (something grilled or a vegetable dish) you may be lured by one of the luscious chocolate-based desserts. If the meal has been rich and copiously sauced, you might prefer one of the fruit-based puddings, ranging from home-made ice creams based on fruit purées (no fancy machinery needed) to tarts or mousses.

Meringues are another good option, especially if you have made a fruit ice cream with egg yolks and need a home for the whites. They are easy to make, lend themselves to all kinds of embroidery and can be prepared ahead. And bearing in mind that, as Jane Austen claimed, 'good apple pies are a considerable part of domestic happiness', there are several variations on that theme.

Some of the puddings are frozen or cold, others are warm. Best of all are those that combine the two elements to give a wonderful contrast.

DELICIOUS *desserts*

White Chocolate Mousse (Basic Recipe)

Here is a master recipe which can be served nature *in coupes or demitasse coffee cups, with a little grated bitter chocolate on top or with fresh fruit (especially wild strawberries). Or it can be spooned into brandy snap baskets, or set on dark chocolate hearts made from melted, cooled chocolate – see the 2 recipes that follow.*

Serves 8-10

50g (1¾oz) **caster sugar**

2 sheets **gelatine**, soaked in cold water or 1 teaspoon powdered gelatine sprinkled onto 3 tablespoons cold water

200g (7oz) **white chocolate**

500ml (18fl oz) **whipping cream**

Put the sugar in a heavy-based saucepan with 6 tablespoons cold water, heat gently, stirring until dissolved, then increase the heat and boil for about 5 minutes to make a bubbling syrup.

Remove the pan from the heat, squeeze out the gelatine sheets and drop them into the pan. Alternatively, add the sponged-up, powdered gelatine to the pan. Stir until dissolved, then set aside.

Break up the white chocolate and put it in a heatproof bowl with 3 tablespoons of the cream. Set the bowl over a pan of barely simmering water – the bottom of the bowl should not touch the water – and allow the chocolate to melt, stirring gently with a wooden spoon until smooth. Remove from the heat and stir in the melted gelatine mixture with a wire whisk. Set aside and allow to cool to room temperature.

Whip the remaining cream in a bowl until it forms fairly stiff peaks. Fold two tablespoons of the cream into the chocolate mixture to loosen it up, then tip all the chocolate into the bowl of cream, lifting and folding with a wire whisk until the cream is mixed in. Spoon into individual serving dishes or coffee cups and chill until set.

White Chocolate Mousse in Brandy Snap Baskets

A White Chocolate Mousse is set in thoroughly British brandy snap baskets and served with a Red Fruit Coulis for a nice, sharp contrast. It's a recipe that goes down well in foreign parts – the sort of places where people are not familiar with the wonders of brandy snaps. (As all good ex-pats know, runny honey is an excellent substitute for golden syrup.)

Serves 8

FOR THE BRANDY SNAP BASKETS

50g (1¾oz) **butter**

50g (1¾oz) **soft light brown sugar**

50g (1¾oz) **golden syrup**

50g (1¾oz) **plain flour,** *sifted*

a pinch of salt

1 teaspoon **lemon juice**

1 teaspoon **ground ginger**

1 quantity
white chocolate mousse
(see recipe on page 172)

red fruit coulis
(see recipe on page 184),
to serve

Line a large, heavy baking sheet with non-stick baking parchment and set aside. Preheat the oven to 180°C/350°F/Gas Mark 4. For the brandy snap baskets, put the butter with the sugar and golden syrup in a saucepan and heat gently until melted and blended, stirring. Remove the pan from the heat, stir in the flour, salt, lemon juice and ginger and mix thoroughly.

Place 4 blobs (each about a tablespoonful) of the mixture, well-spaced out, on the prepared baking sheet and spread the mixture out as thinly as possible with the back of a wetted metal spoon to give a circle each about 12cm (4½in) in diameter.

Bake in the oven for about 8 minutes or until golden brown, full of holes and bubbly. Do not allow them to get too brown or they will be hard to work with. Remove from the oven and while they are still warm, lift them off the sheet with a spatula and drape them over upturned glasses or dariole moulds to give a cupped shape. Leave until hard before lifting off.

Make, bake and shape 4 more in the same way with the remaining mixture. The shaped cups will stay fresh and crispy for a few hours at room temperature; for a longer wait, store them in an airtight tin.

Make the white chocolate mousse and spoon some of the mousse into each basket. Refrigerate until firm. Serve each filled basket on a pool of fruit coulis.

White Chocolate Mousse on Dark Chocolate Bases

Dark chocolate is melted, spread into rounds (or heart shapes, for Valentine's Day) and cooled until firm. The White Chocolate Mousse is spooned into ovals on top. Serve with a fruit coulis and some fresh fruit, too, if you like.

Trace eight circles or hearts (about 10cm/4in in diameter or at their widest point) onto sheets of non-stick baking parchment and set aside.

Break up the dark chocolate and put it in a heatproof bowl. Set the bowl over a pan of simmering water and leave until the chocolate has melted, or melt the chocolate in a microwave oven, according to the manufacturer's instructions.

Using a palette knife, spread about 1 tablespoon melted chocolate smoothly inside each circle or heart on the parchment on a flat work surface, going well to the edges. Work quickly so that the chocolate remains liquid. Cool the circles or hearts until hardened. Make the white chocolate mousse and chill until set.

To serve, peel the chocolate circles or hearts off the parchment and put them on serving plates. Dip a nice, deeply oval dessertspoon into a jug of warm water and spoon out ovals of mousse. Arrange two ovals of mousse on top of each chocolate circle or heart. Serve over a fruit coulis or with fresh fruit and decorate with mint sprigs.

Serves 8

150g (5½oz)
dark chocolate

1 quantity
white chocolate mousse
(see recipe on page 172)

fruit coulis or *fresh fruit*, to serve

fresh **mint** *sprigs, to decorate*

Black and White Mischief in an Almond Crumb Crust with a Raspberry Coulis

A monstrously rich and wonderful dessert consisting of both dark and white chocolate mousses on a nutty crumb base. It's a bit of a production, but it's worth it – and it can be prepared several days ahead. For a larger cake, serving 12, double all the quantities and mould it in a 26cm (10½in) springform tin. The raspberry coulis makes a nice sharp contrast.

Preheat the oven to 200°C/400°F/Gas Mark 6. Crush the biscuits in a food processor, add the almonds and melted butter and process briefly to mix. Press the mixture firmly into the bottom of an 18cm (7in) springform cake tin which is 5-6cm (2-2½in) deep. Bake the biscuit crust in the oven for 6-8 minutes or until lightly golden. Set aside to cool.

Put the dark chocolate in one heatproof bowl and the white chocolate in another. Add 3 tablespoons of cream to each. Set each bowl over a pan of barely simmering water and allow the chocolate to melt very gently. Remove from the heat and stir the chocolates until smooth and glossy, then allow them to cool. Whip the remaining cream in a bowl until stiff, divide it equally between the cooled chocolates and fold in carefully using a wire whisk. Spoon half the white chocolate mousse over the crumb crust in the tin. Top with all the dark chocolate mousse. Finish with the remaining white chocolate mousse. Smooth the top. Chill the cake for at least 6 hours and up to 48 hours.

For the coulis, purée the raspberries and sugar to taste in a blender or food processor until smooth. Add the kirsch, if using, blend, then add a little water and blend to give a pouring consistency. Pour into a jug and set aside.

Just before serving, set the cake in its springform tin on a cake rack. Sift some cocoa powder over the top, then lift the cake onto a plate and release it from its brace. Decorate with mint sprigs and serve with the raspberry coulis.

Serves 6

50g (1¾oz) **lightly sweetened plain biscuits** such as digestive or petit beurre

3 tablespoons **ground almonds**

50g (1¾oz) **butter**, melted and cooled

100g (3½oz) best quality **dark chocolate** such as Lindt Surfin or Terry's Bitter

100g (3½oz) **white chocolate**

300ml (½ pint) **whippingcream**, plus 6 tablespoons

FOR THE COULIS

250g (9oz) **raspberries**

caster sugar, to taste

1 tablespoon **Kirsch** (optional)

cocoa powder, for dusting

fresh **mint** sprigs, to decorate

A Basic Fruit Ice

An all-purpose ice cream based on a thick fruit purée, a mousse of whipped egg yolks, sugar syrup and whipped cream. The recipe may be adapted to use all kinds of fruit; you need about 400ml (14fl oz) fruit purée. Some fruits (such as raspberries, strawberries, peaches, nectarines, pears and bananas) may be puréed raw; others (such as blackberries, blackcurrants, apples and rhubarb) will need to be cooked before puréeing. The amount of sugar added to the purée will also vary depending on the fruit used – start with 50g (1¾oz) and add more if necessary, bearing in mind that the egg yolk base is also sweetened.

Serves 6

500g (1lb 2oz) prepared fruit, such as blackberries

50g-100g (1¾-3½oz) caster sugar

1 tablespoon **crème de mûre** or crème de cassis (optional)

100g (3½oz) **caster sugar**

3 **egg yolks**

250ml (9fl oz) **whipping cream**

For the fruit purée, put the fruit in a pan with sugar to taste (see notes above). Bring to the boil and bubble gently for a few minutes until the juices run – do not overcook. Push the fruit through a sieve into a bowl. Discard the pips. Stir the liqueur, if using, into the fruit purée. Taste to see if it is sweet enough – if not, add more sugar. You should have about 400ml (14fl oz) purée. Allow to cool.

For the mousse, put 100ml (3½fl oz) water in a saucepan with the sugar. Heat gently, stirring, until dissolved, then bring to the boil and boil steadily for about 5 minutes or until the syrup reaches the thread stage: to test this, dip a fork into the syrup and let it cool a little. Pinch some of the syrup repeatedly between index finger and thumb. As you separate finger and thumb, the syrup should form a thread.

Beat the egg yolks briefly in a mixing bowl and pour on the hot syrup. Continue beating until the mixture becomes pale, fluffy and mousse-like.

In a separate bowl, whip the cream until softly stiff. Fold together the fruit purée, egg mixture and whipped cream, mixing well. Spoon the mixture into a cling-wrap-lined loaf tin, pudding bowl or individual moulds. Freeze until firm.

Remove the ice cream from the freezer to the fridge about 1 hour before serving. Serve with slices of fresh fruit, or wild strawberries, or in brandy snap baskets.

Personal Summer Puddings

These make stunning dinner party pieces, guaranteed to delight any guests who may be unfamiliar with the joys of summer pudding. For the uninitiated, these are little castles made with white bread and a mixture of soft fruits, moulded in ramekins and turned out for serving. It's important to use thinly sliced, slightly stale white bread – the small round slices designed to make canapés are ideal. The puddings should be made at least 1 day (better still, 2 days) ahead if possible, so that the juices penetrate the bread thoroughly.

Take 6 ramekin dishes, each 7-8cm (2¾-3¼in) in diameter. Cut out 6 rounds of bread and put into the bases of the dishes. Cut the other bread slices into 3 equal strips each, and use them to line the sides of the dishes. Set aside.

Put the fruit in a saucepan with the blackcurrant leaves, if using, the sugar and 125ml (4fl oz) water. Bring to a gentle boil, stirring occasionally, then simmer for about 5 minutes or until the juices run.

Remove the pan from the heat and fish out and discard the blackcurrant leaves, if used. Add the squeezed-out gelatine sheets (or the sponged-up gelatine) to the fruit mixture and stir until dissolved. Crush the fruit roughly with a potato masher, then stir in the crème de cassis, if using. Allow the fruit to cool.

Spoon some fruit into the bottom of the bread-lined ramekins. Prick with a fork to make sure the juices penetrate the bottom slices. Fill with the remaining fruit. Run a knife around between the bread and the edge of the ramekins and press down to ensure that the juices penetrate thoroughly. Chill for at least 24 hours, better still, 48 hours, before serving.

To serve, run a knife round the ramekins and turn them out onto plates. Serve with single cream, Greek yoghurt, a red fruit coulis or ice cream and scatter some wild strawberries or raspberries around the puddings, to decorate.

Serves 6

12 thin slices **white bread**, slightly stale, crusts removed

2 sheets **gelatine** soaked in cold water, or 1 teaspoon powdered gelatine sprinkled onto 3 tablespoons cold water

500g (1lb 2oz) **assorted soft fruit** such as raspberries, blackcurrants, redcurrants and strawberries

a few fresh **blackcurrant leaves** (optional)

100g (3½oz) **caster sugar**

1 tablespoon **crème de cassis** (optional)

wild strawberries or raspberries, to decorate

A Seriously Good Chocolate Cake

A seriously good chocolate cake has to taste seriously of chocolate, should have little or no flour, and probably some ground almonds for moisture. The quality of the chocolate is paramount: choose one with a high cocoa content – at least 52%. Best of all are those with 70%.

The cake must be prepared ahead – up to 2 days, in order for the flavours to mellow. It stays wonderfully moist and it freezes well. Set it on a white plate and serve in small wedges.

Makes 12–24 slices

150g (5½oz) top-quality **dark chocolate** (see note above)

125g (4½oz) **butter**, diced

6 **eggs**, separated

150g (5½oz) **ground almonds**

1 tablespoon **framboise, kirsch** or **Cointreau** (optional)

a pinch of salt

75g (2¾oz) **caster sugar**

Preheat the oven to 170°C/325°F/Gas Mark 3. Cut a disc of non-stick baking parchment to fit the bottom of a 26cm (10½in) springform tin. Butter and flour the sides of the tin and knock away any excess flour, then put the parchment disc in the base of the tin. Set aside.

Break the chocolate into squares and melt it with the butter in a heavy-based saucepan over a very gentle heat, stirring until smooth. Remove the pan from the heat and stir in the egg yolks, ground almonds and liqueur, if using. Set aside.

Put the egg whites in a large mixing bowl with the salt. Beat them until they hold soft peaks. Still beating, sprinkle on the sugar in a steady stream. Beat for a few minutes more to make a meringue-like consistency. Spoon two tablespoons of whites into the chocolate-almond mixture, then carefully cut and fold in the rest.

Transfer the mixture to the prepared tin and smooth the top. Bake the cake in the oven for 30-35 minutes or until a little risen (don't expect anything dramatic – this is not a high-performance cake, just a seriously good one). It should be just firm to the touch and no longer wobbly when nudged, but it should be underdone – its role in life is to be moist.

Remove from the oven and cool the cake in the tin, then release the springform and set a cake rack on top. Invert the cake onto the rack and peel away and discard the bottom paper. Put the cake on a plate and decorate.

Frozen Hazelnut Meringue with Blackberry Ice Cream

Here's a wonderful way to make something special with the Basic Fruit Ice recipe on page 178: thin sheets of hazelnut meringue are sandwiched together with blackberry (or other) ice cream and frozen. The timing is a bit tricky – you have to catch the ice cream before it freezes too hard, otherwise it will be difficult to spread over the meringue sheets. If you use bought ice cream, bring it from the freezer to the fridge for an hour or two before using, to soften it up.

Make the ice cream according to the recipe on page 178. Put it in the freezer while you make the meringues.

Draw 3 circles about 20cm (8in) in diameter on 3 sheets of non-stick baking parchment and place them on baking sheets. Set aside. Preheat the oven to 150°C/300°F/Gas Mark 2.

In a bowl, beat the egg whites with the salt until foaming. Add the sugar in a steady stream and continue beating until the mixture is snowy white and firm. Carefully fold in the hazelnuts. Divide the mixture equally among the 3 sheets of parchment, spreading it out carefully to the edges of the marked circles – it will be quite thin.

Bake the meringues in the oven for 30-40 minutes or until they are lightly browned and no longer stick to the parchment. Remove from the parchment and put on wire racks to cool.

Lay one of the meringue rounds in the bottom of a 22cm (8½in) springform cake tin. Spread half the soft ice cream over the meringue round. Place a second meringue round on top, add the rest of the ice cream and top with the last meringue round – be careful as the meringues are very fragile. Freeze the dessert for several hours before serving.

To serve, release the springform and set the dessert on a beautiful plate. Decorate with fresh fruit and mint sprigs.

Serves 6

1 quantity (about 1 litre/1¾ pints) **blackberry ice cream** *(see recipe on page 178)* or other fruit ice cream

3 **egg whites**

a pinch of salt

150g (5½oz) **caster sugar**

75g (2¾oz) **ground hazelnuts**

fresh fruit and fresh **mint** sprigs, to decorate

Lemon and Lime Ice Cream with Almond Tuiles

A rich, but not overly sweet, ice cream on a juice base, one of my mother's best recipes (another was for Yorkshire Puddings, see recipe on page 40). Use left-over egg whites from the ice cream to make the almond tuiles (see recipe below) to accompany the ice, or make them into meringue for a Lemon and Lime Ice Cream Meringue Torte (see recipe on opposite page).

Serves 6

FOR THE ICE CREAM

150g (5½oz) **caster sugar**

6 **egg yolks**

juice of 2 **lemons** and 2 **limes** (about 150ml/¼ pint), strained

300ml (½ pint) **whipping cream**

FOR THE ALMOND TUILES

2 **egg whites**, lightly beaten

75g (2¾oz) **caster sugar**

50g (1¾oz) **flaked almonds**

2 tablespoons **plain flour**

finely grated zest of 1 **lemon**

fresh **mint** sprigs or pieces or strips of lime zest, blanched, to decorate

For the ice cream, make a syrup by dissolving the sugar gently in 3 tablespoons water in a saucepan, then boil the mixture briskly for 5 minutes until a little thickened. Remove the pan from the heat.

In a bowl, beat together the egg yolks and sugar syrup until they lighten and thicken considerably. Stir in the lemon and lime juice.

In a separate bowl, whip the cream until stiff, then fold it into the egg yolk mixture. Freeze the ice cream in a bowl or other suitable container for several hours, until firm.

For the almond tuiles, line a baking sheet with non-stick baking parchment and set aside. Preheat the oven to 200°C/400°F/Gas Mark 6. Put the egg whites, sugar and almonds in a bowl and mix together gently with a fork. Sift the flour into the mixture and work it in gently, then stir in the grated lemon zest.

Put 6 teaspoonful-sized blobs of the mixture, well-spaced out, onto the prepared baking sheet. Dip a fork into cold water and flatten the mixture with the back of the fork. The tuiles should be very thin.

Bake in the oven for about 8 minutes or until golden brown. Lift them off the paper and cool on a wire rack. Repeat with the remaining mixture until it is all used up.

To serve, spoon ovals of the ice cream onto the almond tuiles (2-3 per person) on plates and decorate with mint sprigs or blanched lime zest.

Ice Cream Meringue Torte

Another way to present the gorgeous lemon and lime ice cream (see previous page) is to sandwich it between two meringue discs and freeze until firm. Garnish with redcurrant sprays and a few leaves for colour.

Use a 26cm (10in) springform cake tin to trace two circles on baking parchment. You will need the tin to shape the torte when you are assembling the layers.

Make the meringue mixture as describe on page 184. and divide it between the two circles, spreading it out smoothly to the edges. Bake as directed.

When the meringues are done, lift them off the paper and put one in the bottom of the springform tin. Make the ice cream and pour it into the tin. Top with the second meringue disc and freeze the torte.

To serve, release the springform tin and set the torte on your best plate. Decorate with a few delicate redcurrant sprigs and leaves.

Serves 10

FOR THE MERINGUE
3 egg whites
a pinch of salt
150g (5½oz) **caster sugar**
1 teaspoon **cornflower**
1 teaspoon
white wine vinegar
1 quantity **lemon and lime ice cream**
(see recipe on opposite page)
fresh **redcurrant** *sprigs and leaves, to garnish*

Meringue Rounds with Fresh Fruit on a Red Fruit Coulis

A stunning dessert, light and sharp after a rich meal: meringue rounds covered with a selection of fresh fruit and served over a red fruit coulis. The meringue rounds can be prepared a few days ahead (or frozen, for a longer wait), the fruit prepared a few hours before serving and refrigerated, and the coulis puréed and strained. Assemble at the last moment.

Serves 8

FOR THE MERINGUE
ROUNDS WITH FRUIT

3 egg whites

a pinch of salt

150g (5½oz) caster sugar

1 teaspoon cornflour

1 teaspoon
white wine vinegar

1 pink-fleshed grapefruit

2 oranges

2 kiwi fruit

4-5 kumquats

2 bananas

FOR THE FRUIT COULIS

500g (1lb 2oz)
raspberries or
strawberries

caster sugar, to taste

1 tablespoon kirsch
(optional)

fresh mint leaves or
fresh pineapple sage
flowers, to decorate

For the meringues, draw four 10cm (4in) diameter circles on 2 sheets of non-stick baking parchment and place on baking sheets. Preheat the oven to 110°C/225°F/Gas Mark ¼.

Beat the whites and salt together in a bowl using an electric mixer to form soft peaks. Mix the sugar and cornflour together, and add these to the egg whites in a steady stream; continue beating until the mixture becomes stiff and glossy. Mix in the vinegar.

Divide the meringue mixture equally among the 8 circles. Spread it out smoothly with a spatula to the edges of the circles, wetting the spatula regularly so the meringue doesn't stick to it.

Bake the meringues in the oven for about 1 hour or until they are just dried out – they should not colour, and when ready they will lift off the paper. Remove from the paper and put on wire racks to cool.

Peel the grapefruit and oranges à vif (down to the flesh, leaving no white pith) with a very sharp knife. Cut the segments out of the membranes which encase and divide them. Peel and slice the kiwi fruit and slice the kumquats very thinly, leaving the skin intact. Put all the prepared fruit on a plate or in a bowl, cover with cling wrap and refrigerate (leave the bananas until the last minute before peeling and slicing them and adding them to the rest of the prepared fruit).

For the coulis, purée the raspberries or strawberries in a blender or food processor with sugar to taste, keeping the flavour quite sharp. Push the purée through a sieve into a bowl and discard the pips. Stir in the kirsch, if using, then add enough cold water to make a pouring consistency. Cover and chill the coulis.

Just before serving, pour a little coulis onto each plate. Put a meringue round on top, arrange a selection of prepared fresh fruit on each meringue and decorate with mint leaves or pineapple sage flowers.

Swiss Apple Tart with Hazelnuts

The Swiss understand about good apple tarts. Here is an especially fine one consisting of grated apple mixed with ground nuts, sugar and butter.

Serves 8

300g (10½oz) ready-made **shortcrust pastry**

1kg (2¼lb) non-collapsing **eating apples**, such as Cox's or Braeburn, peeled, cored and grated

100g (3½oz) **ground hazelnuts** or ground almonds

50g (1¾oz) **caster sugar**

finely grated zest and juice of 1 **lemon**

25g (1oz) chilled **butter**, cut into dots

Preheat the oven to 200°C/400°F/Gas Mark 6 and put a heavy black baking sheet on the shelf nearest the floor of the oven. Roll out the pastry on a lightly floured surface and use it to line a 30cm (12in) loose-bottomed quiche tin. Chill it while you prepare the filling.

Put the grated apples, half the ground nuts, the sugar and lemon zest and juice in a large bowl and mix well. Spread the remaining ground nuts in the pastry case. Spoon the apple mixture over the nuts and scatter the butter dots on top.

Bake the tart on top of the baking sheet in the oven for 10 minutes or until the base of the pastry is just cooked through. Move the tart, on the baking sheet, to the top of the oven and reduce the oven temperature to180°C/350°F/Gas Mark 4. Continue baking the tart for a further 20-25 minutes or until the edges of the pastry and the filling are nicely golden. Serve tepid with ice cream.

Honey and Greek Yoghurt Mousse with Soft Fruits

A soothing mousse, softly set with gelatine. Your choice of honey will dictate how interesting it tastes. Bog-standard honey from undefined sources may result in something a bit dull – try acacia honey or lavender honey (subtle and fragrant) or a robust, dark honeydew honey for a more assertive result.

Soak the sheet gelatine in cold water in a bowl until floppy. Alternatively, sprinkle the powdered gelatine onto 3 tablespoons water in a cup and leave until sponged up. Put the squeezed-out or soaked gelatine in a small saucepan with the honey and 3 tablespoons of the cream. Dissolve the gelatine over a gentle heat, stirring, without allowing it to boil. Remove the pan from the heat and stir to ensure even dissolution. Set aside and allow to cool to lukewarm.

In a bowl, whip the remaining cream until it forms soft peaks, and set aside. Put the Greek yoghurt in a blender or food processor and add the cooled but still liquid gelatine mixture. Blend until smooth and well mixed, then pour into a bowl. Fold the cream into this mixture with a wire whisk, lifting and folding to blend everything smoothly.

Lightly oil a charlotte mould 8cm (3¼in) high and 14cm (5½in) top diameter or similar size and line it with cling wrap (or use another tin of similar capacity, such as a straight-sided cake tin or loaf tin). Pour in the mousse mixture. Alternatively, pour the mousse into lined ramekins or dariole moulds for individual servings. Or, if your nerve fails you, simply pour the mousse into your best crystal bowl and spoon it out into neat ovals for serving. Put in the refrigerator to set for at least 4 hours, before serving.

Turn (or spoon) the mousse(s) out onto plates, serve with a selection of seasonal soft fruits and decorate with fresh lavender sprigs.

Serves 6-8

4 sheets of **gelatine** or
3 teaspoons powdered
gelatine

100g (3½oz) **honey**
(see notes above)

300ml (½ pint)
whipping cream

200g (7oz)
Greek yoghurt

a selection of
seasonal soft fruits
such as wild strawberries
and raspberries, to serve

fresh **lavender** sprigs,
to decorate

Puff Pastry Wheels with Apple Spokes

Puff pastry is rolled out wafer-thin and cut into discs, adorned with thinly sliced apples arranged like the spokes of a wheel, scattered with butter dots and sprinkled with brown sugar. The beauty of this dessert is that the pastries can be prepared in advance and frozen, then baked straight from the freezer. Serve each with a scoop of vanilla ice cream.

Serves 8

300g (10½oz) ready-made **puff pastry**

4 well-flavoured, non-collapsing **eating apples** such as Cox's or Braeburn

lemon juice, to sprinkle

dots of **butter**, to scatter

light soft brown sugar, to sprinkle

8 scoops of **vanilla ice cream**

ground cinnamon, to sprinkle

8 toasted **hazelnuts**, to decorate (see note below)

Line 2-3 baking sheets with non-stick baking parchment and set aside. Preheat the oven to 220°C/425°F/Gas Mark 7. Cut the puff pastry into 8 equal-sized pieces. Roll each piece out thinly to a rough circle, on a lightly floured surface. Invert a 15cm (6in) saucer or small plate over each pastry circle and cut out a disc. Place the pastry discs on the prepared baking sheets and set aside.

Peel, quarter and core the apples. Cut each apple into very thin slices (aim for about 36 slices from each apple, otherwise they are not thin enough). Arrange them like the spokes of a wheel, slightly overlapping and domed up in the centre, on the pastry discs. Sprinkle with lemon juice, scatter dots of butter on top and sprinkle with brown sugar. Chill (or open freeze) them on the baking sheets if they are not to be cooked immediately.

Bake the pastries in the oven for 10-15 minutes or until the pastry is golden and cooked through and the apples are golden. Put a scoop of ice cream in the middle of each pastry, sprinkle with cinnamon, decorate each with a chopped toasted hazelnut and serve.

For toasted hazelnuts (keep a stock in the freezer for decorating desserts), put shelled hazelnuts on a baking sheet in a preheated oven at 200°C/400°F/Gas Mark 6. Toast the nuts for 15-20 minutes, until golden and fragrant. Cool, then roughly rub off the husks (if you use freshly shelled hazelnuts, there is no need to rub off the husks after toasting). Freeze in cartons until needed.

Index